Starting Off Right
in Law School

Starting Off Right
in Law School

Carolyn J. Nygren

CAROLINA ACADEMIC PRESS
Durham, North Carolina

Library of Congress Cataloging-in-Publication Data

Nygren, Carolyn, 1942–
    Starting off right in law school / by Carolyn Nygren.
        p.   cm.
    ISBN 0-89089-877-4
    1. Law — Study and teaching — United States.   I. Title
KF273.N97   1997
340'.071'173 — DC21   97-12484
                                                              CIP

Carolina Academic Press
700 Kent Street
Durham, NC 27701
Telephone (919) 489-7486
Fax (919) 493-5668
Email www.cap-press.com

Printed in the United States of America

Table of Contents

Introduction

Why I Wrote This Book

1. To provide information about the legal system

Law schools do not require that their entering students have any specific knowledge of the law. Unfortunately, in order to understand their assignments for the first day of law school, students need to be familiar with fundamental legal principles and legal terminology as well as know information about the court systems and the trial and appellate processes. Students at most law schools must spend a great deal of time during the first semester trying to fill in the gaps in their basic knowledge at the same time that they are trying to cope with their course work. No wonder that most are exhausted and discouraged.

Students do not need in-depth knowledge of the legal system to be ready for the first day of law school. There are three years to learn the details. They just need the basics. The first reason I wrote this book is to provide those essential basics.

2. To provide information about the study skills necessary for success

When I first started working at law schools, I was hired to work in the Spring with students who had not done well on first semester exams. I soon realized that most of the students had worked very hard and had learned enough law to do well. What they hadn't learned was that law school exams are different from any other exams they had taken and doing well requires some specific study and exam preparation techniques. Unless told otherwise, students who have had success in other academic settings have no reason to believe that they need to study differently in law school. Sometimes it is not until they do poorly on first semester exams that they understand that they need help.

Most students can be successful if they know what preparation is required. Therefore, the second reason for writing this book is to tell students about study and exam preparation techniques before their first exams. All students should know how to demonstrate what they have learned.

Why You Should Read This Book

First year success is more important to law students than to students in any other graduate program. Selection for law review is often dependent on grades. Law firms are usually conservative and often rely almost exclusively on grades to determine to whom to make an offer. Therefore, some very promising students are cut off from opportunities simply because they do not know how to succeed in law school. This book contains what you need to know so that you can do well enough in law school to achieve your goals.

What You Should Know About the Book

The "Voices"

This book is based on a course I taught for many years. The chapters that contain basic law related information rarely include the word "I." However, the chapters that contain study and exam preparation techniques are based on my experience in teaching and working with individual students. In these chapters I often refer to suggestions that have worked for me and others, and I also include samples from the course.

The Topic

When you read the book, you may be surprised by the fact that the events that resulted in the cases being tried are rather mundane. All of the cases you will read are about people who have been injured by something in food, either in their restaurant meals or in processed food. You will read about people who have been injured by a bone in fish chowder, a bone in a fish fillet, and even a pearl in canned oysters. The injured parties are all suing the merchants who sold them the food under one legal theory found in the Uniform Commercial Code called the implied warranty of merchantability.

You should know that the case at the heart of this book (*Webster v. Blue Ship Tea Room, Inc.*) created problems for generations of Massachusetts lawyers as you will see in Chapter One. In 1989 the Supreme Judicial Court decided a case which clarified the unresolved issues in *Webster*. However, this action by the court did not decrease the effectiveness of *Webster* as a teaching tool nor its appeal to law school teachers and students.

The reason I have chosen such an easy subject is that I want you to be able to concentrate on learning about the law. All of us have eaten in restaurants and consumed canned or frozen food from the supermarket. Although the subject matter is easy, the legal concepts in the cases are not, and there are many scholarly articles written about what one such article calls "chicken bone law."

The Simplified Explanations

Some legal concepts may seem clear in this book because they are introduced in only one area. In your first year courses, you may find that they are quite complex. However, it is impossible to understand the complexities at the beginning of your law school experience. Now you need a basic understanding of legal concepts and vocabulary so that you can have the foundation upon which to build a more sophisticated understanding. This book is meant to give you enough of an introduction to the law and law school so that you can begin speaking and writing like a member of the legal community immediately.

Acknowledgments

I am indebted to H. Peter Klein and David M. Prentiss for their encouragement and to Greta Strittmatter of Carolina Academic Press for her patience.

Starting Off Right
in Law School

The Sources of Law

Background for this Chapter

Most of this chapter is the story of the beginning stages of a law suit. This background section comes first so that the story can be told without interruptions to explain legal terms. In many instances the explanations of the terms are simplified, but they are sufficient for this introductory book and your first days in law school.

You will encounter many words in law school that are unfamiliar to you or are used in ways that are unfamiliar to you. Therefore, the purchase of a legal dictionary designed for law students is wise. Although you will later want to own the famous lawyers' dictionary, *Black's Law Dictionary*, many first year students are as confused by the definitions in *Black's* as they are by the terms they look up.

Court

1. Court can mean one of the institutions of our legal system. For example, "Oliver James is taking his former employee John Lewis to court because he believes that Mr. Lewis violated their non-competition agreement."

Most states have a three tier court system. The role of the judges of the first tier courts (the trial courts) is to apply existing law to the disputes they hear. The primary role of the judges of the second tier courts is to correct errors made by the judges in the trial courts. The role of the judges of the third tier is to make law. The second and third tier courts are called appellate courts. This system of state courts will be described in more detail at the beginning of Chapter 2. The federal system (not described in the book) has a three tier structure.

2. Court also can mean the judges who make the decisions about the disputes. For example, "The court found that a bone in a bowl of fish chowder did not make the chowder unmerchantable," means that in the document written to issue a decision, the judges or judge stated that a bone in fish chowder did not make the chowder unmerchantable. This is the most frequent use of the term "court" in this book.

Statute

A statute is a law made by a legislature. Statutes are enacted in order to regulate people's future conduct. Although most law school courses allot little time to statutes, many of the problems of a lawyer's clients are addressed in statutes.

Judge-Made Law

Although many people think of the "law" as statutes only, decisions of judges about disputes are also law. Judge-made law results from a decision rendered by a court in a particular case. Even when the source of law is a statute, parties often must go to court to obtain clarification of the meaning of a word in the statute.

Case

1. Case can mean the controversy that has brought the parties to the legal system. (Attorney Smith is working on a difficult case.)

2. Case also can mean the document that a judge writes to record the outcome of a trial and to state the reasons for the outcome. (I just read a difficult case.) The word "opinion" is often used interchangeably with "case."

Stare Decisis and Precedent

Cases are so important because of two related concepts of our legal system: stare decisis and precedent. Stare decisis (Latin for "stand by the decision") means that the decision of a court in one case provides a precedent (a standard) for how future cases are decided. If a later case has like facts and issues to the earlier one, it must be decided in the same way as the earlier one if it is in the same court or lower courts. Cases decided in one state are binding precedent only in that state.

Plaintiff and Defendant

The party first bringing a case is called the "plaintiff," and the party being sued is called the "defendant." However, you may not be able to determine which is which in an appellate case. Many states use the name of the plaintiff as the first name in the title of the case at all levels. Others order the names so that the name of the party appealing is first. The party appealing is the "appellant," and the other party is the "appellee."

Cause of Action

The alleged facts of any dispute must satisfy the requirements of some cause of action (legal theory) before the dispute can be resolved by a court. For example, in most states a cause of action for battery requires that someone (1) intentionally (2) touch another person (3) in a hostile or offensive manner (4) without permission and (5) with no defense. If any one of these elements does not exist, there is no cause of action in battery.

The reason people bring disputes into the legal system is to obtain a remedy for a wrong. The most common remedy the legal system provides is "damages" (money). Damages are awarded when the defendant is found responsible for the wrong and therefore "liable" to the plaintiff under some cause of action.

Defense

1. Defense can mean any fact or legal argument which would make the defendant not liable (or guilty in a criminal trial) even if all the facts alleged by the plaintiff were true. (Assumption of the risk is a defense in a warranty case.)

2. Defense also can mean the conduct of trial on behalf of the defendant. (The defense rests.)

Jurisdiction

1. Jurisdiction can mean a particular legal system—usually based on geography. (Ohio and Maine are different jurisdictions.)

2. Jurisdiction also can mean the power to hear a case. (Ohio, not Maine, has jurisdiction in this case.)

Reporter

Reporters are books in which the cases of a jurisdiction are printed in chronological order. One state reporter is the official document published by the state. However, few lawyers use this reporter because it contains only the official language of the opinion. Most lawyers use one of the unofficial reporters published by the West Publishing Company because the West editors use an indexing system which is extremely helpful to lawyers.

Each state has a reporter in which the opinions of the highest state are published. Some reporters contain the opinions of the second tier courts as well. West also publishes regional reporters including the major cases from several states. The regional reporter referred to later in this chapter is the *North Eastern Reporter* which contains cases from Illinois, Indiana, Massachusetts, New York and Ohio. The reporter system will be explained in detail in every law school's course in legal research and writing, and you should not be concerned with the details now.

Uniform Commercial Code (UCC)

The UCC is a proposal for legislation drafted by national experts in commercial law. The legislatures of all states have incorporated the UCC into their statutes (Louisiana partially). Because the basic law is the same in all states, courts often cite cases from other states in their opinions as "persuasive" precedent. The state statutes retain the section number of the original document so cross referencing cases is easy.

The Filet of Flounder
with Lobster Sauce

Telling the Story

Nelson Palmer was eating his tuna fish sandwich and studying a client's file when a distraught Margaret Fox called.

"Nelson, I want to sue that Fearless Flounder restaurant," she said in a voice that Mr. Palmer recognized as being raspy and softer than usual.

"Okay Margaret, tell me all about it," Mr. Palmer replied. Ms. Fox had been his client for five years, and he knew she sometimes had a temper.

"I just bought the first new car I've ever owned, and Paul took me to The Fearless Flounder last night to celebrate. I've never been so scared in my life. I ordered my favorite dish, filet of flounder with lobster sauce. Paul had bought an expensive bottle of champagne, and we were having a wonderful time. Suddenly, I felt as if something was stuck in my throat. I could still breathe, but every time I swallowed it hurt. I didn't want to embarrass myself so I went into the ladies room to see if I could get rid of whatever was there. I tried reaching down my throat, but I couldn't get to anything. I finally went back to the table and mentioned my problem to the waitress. She brought me some bread and milk, but after I ate them I still felt something stuck. I managed to finish my meal, but our celebration was certainly ruined. Paul paid the bill and we went back to my apartment. After about an hour I got so uncomfortable Paul took me to the hospital. This morning I had some minor operation that I can't pronounce. I knew there was something very wrong. They found a small bone. I'll be all right, but my throat is very sore. How dare the restaurant sell unsafe food!"

While Ms. Fox was talking, Mr. Palmer was analyzing the situation. He thought he remembered from his Contracts and Commercial Law courses that one of the warranties in the Uniform Commercial Code (UCC) section on Sales protected purchasers of food. He knew he'd better be sure before he said anything to his client.

"Let me do some quick research, Margaret, and I'll get back to you later today."

"Okay, but don't take too long. I know how you lawyers like to bill for every minute of your time. Goodbye."

Mr. Palmer sighed, looked suspiciously at his tuna sandwich, put it down, and headed for his book wall.

Deciding to Sue

Mr. Palmer decided to first read an overview of the subject of warranties.

An express warranty is a guarantee by the seller that the service or product he sells conforms to his own description of it, which could be oral, written, a sample, blueprints, or goods sent to the buyer in the past. Leeway is given for the salesman's opinions, sometimes called "puffing." The seller is also held to any express warranty given *after* the sale. Statements such as "This car can go eighty miles per hour, it gets twenty-five miles per gallon, and it has never been in an accident" are all express warranties.

The UCC demands that beyond selling what they say they are selling, merchants adhere to an "implied warranty of merchantability." This is a statutory duty to sell goods fit for the marketplace, which means that they must pass without objection in the trade, be adequately packaged and conform to statements on the label, and be fit for the ordinary purpose for which they are used.

A third warranty under the UCC is the "implied warranty of fitness for a particular purpose," which is given whenever the seller knows of the customer's particular needs, and the customer relies on the seller's knowledge in selecting the proper goods. The seller does not have to be a merchant, and the buyer does not have to tell the seller of his particular needs so long as the seller has reason to know of them and of the customer's reliance on the seller.[1]

Consulting the Statutes

His memory refreshed, Mr. Palmer went to the Massachusetts General Laws where he found the text of Section 2-314 of the Uniform Commercial Code which contains the text of the implied warranty of merchantability.

---

1. Margulies, S. and Lasson, K., Learning Law (1993), pp. 30–31. This book would be a helpful addition to your library of materials to read before starting law school or during your first semester.

"(1) Unless excluded or modified by section 2-316, a warranty that the goods shall be merchantable is implied in a contract for their sale if the seller is a merchant with respect to goods of that kind. Under this section the serving for value of food or drink to be consumed on the premises or elsewhere is a sale."

After determining that "contract for their sale" applies to the present sale of food, Mr. Palmer was certain that the law applied to Ms. Fox's situation. (In everyday language, Section 2-314 says that anytime there is a sale of food by someone who usually sells food, the seller gives the buyer an assurance that the food is merchantable.) Clearly The Fearless Flounder was a "merchant with respect to goods of that kind" (food). Without question, there was a sale. However, what is merchantable food? The definitions of "merchantable" in the UCC seemed hard to apply to food.

Reading a Summary

Mr. Palmer next decided to find some information about how "merchantable" has been interpreted by courts around the country. He looked up Section 2-314 in a legal encyclopedia and read a summary of the status of the law as it applies to food.[2]

Mr. Palmer learned that the law of all states provides that tainted food or food in which a nail or stone is found is unmerchantable. If a merchant sells such food, he or she is liable under the implied warranty of merchantability.

---

2. Mr. Palmer would also look into whether a negligence claim should be considered. If Ms. Fox won her case in negligence, she could recover for her "pain and suffering." Her implied warranty of merchantability claim is a contract claim where only her expenses can be recovered. However, negligence would be very hard to prove here, and Mr. Palmer concentrates on the warranty claim for which he does not have to prove that The Fearless Flounder prepared the food improperly.

However, there is considerable debate about the merchantability of food if the offending substance is a part of the food. Suits have been brought by people who have been injured by a cherry pit in cherry pie, an oyster shell in fried oysters, and an olive pit in a martini olive.

He learned that the cases interpreting merchantability have taken one of two approaches to the problem. The earliest opinions (before the consumer movement) employed the "foreign/natural" test. If the offending substance was natural to the food, the food was merchantable; if not natural to the food, it was unmerchantable.

Recently the "reasonable expectation" test has replaced the "foreign/natural" test in many states. If a person could reasonably expect to find a substance in food, he could take precautions against injury; food sold with such a substance would be considered merchantable. However, if a person could not reasonably expect to find that substance, then the food would be considered unmerchantable.

Consulting the Cases

The official notes to Section 2-314 in the Massachusetts General Laws summarized a case decided by the Supreme Judicial Court in Massachusetts interpreting "merchantability" in which a person was injured eating food in a restaurant. The case Mr. Palmer read is *Webster v. The Blue Ship Tea Room* starting on page 421 of volume 347 of the state reporter and on page 309 of volume 198 of the second edition of the regional reporter (347 Mass. 421, 198 N.E.2d 309).

Mr. Palmer began by looking to the end of the case to see the outcome. The defendant restaurant won, and he was not happy. Because of the doctrine of stare decisis, this case would be binding precedent if the facts were like those of the Fox case. If the facts could not be distinguished, he probably would counsel Ms. Fox against bringing suit. He read the case looking for ways the two cases could be distinguished.

Webster v. Blue Ship Tea Room, Inc.
Supreme Judicial Court of Massachusetts, 1964
198 N.E.2d 309

REARDON, Justice.

This is a case which by its nature evokes earnest study not only of the law but also of the culinary traditions of the Commonwealth which bear so heavily upon its outcome. It is an action to recover damages for personal injuries sustained by reason of a breach of implied warranty of food served by the defendant. . . .

The jury could have found the following facts: On Saturday, April 25, 1959, about 1 P.M., the plaintiff, accompanied by her aunt, entered the Blue Ship Tea Room operated by the defendant. The group was seated at a table and supplied with menus.

This restaurant, which the plaintiff characterized as "quaint," was located in Boston "on the third floor of an old building on T wharf which overlooks the ocean."

The plaintiff, who had been born and brought up in New England (a fact of some consequence), ordered clam chowder and crabmeat salad. Within a few minutes she received tidings to the effect that "there was no more clam chowder," whereupon she ordered a cup of fish chowder. Presently, there was set before her "a small bowl of fish chowder." She had previously enjoyed a breakfast about 9:00 A.M. which had given her no difficulty. "The fish chowder contained haddock, potatoes, milk, water and seasoning. The chowder was milky in color and not clear. The haddock and potatoes were in chunks" (also a fact of consequence). "She agitated it a little with the spoon and observed that it was a fairly full bowl * * *. It was hot when she got it, but she did not tip it with her spoon because it was hot * * * but stirred it in an up and under motion. She denied that she did this because she was looking for something, but it was rather because she wanted an even distribution of fish and potatoes." "She started to eat it, alternating between the chowder and crackers which were on the table with * * * [some] rolls. She ate about 3 or 4 spoonfuls then stopped. She looked at the spoonfuls as she was eating. She saw equal parts of liquid, potato and fish as she spooned it into her mouth. She did not see anything unusual about it. After 3 or 4 spoonfuls she was aware that something had lodged in her throat because she couldn't swallow and couldn't clear her throat by gulping and she could feel it." This misadventure led to two esophago-scopies at the Massachusetts General Hospital, in the second of which, on April 27, 1959, a fish bone was found and removed. The sequence of events produced injury to the plaintiff which was not insubstantial.

We must decide whether a fish bone lurking in a fish chowder, about the ingredients of which there is no other complaint, constitutes a breach of implied warranty under applicable provisions of the Uniform Commercial Code,[1] the annotations to which are not helpful on this point. As the judge put it in his charge, "Was the fish chowder fit to be eaten

---

1. 1 "Unless excluded or modified by section 2-316, a warranty that the goods shall be merchantable is implied in a contract for their sale if the seller is a merchant with respect to goods of that kind. Under this section the serving of food or drink to be consumed either on the premises or elsewhere is a sale. (2) Goods to be merchantable must at least be such as . . . (c) are fit for the ordinary purposes for which such goods are used . . . G.L. c. 106, s 2-314.

" . . . (3)(b) [W]hen the buyer before entering into the contract has examined the goods or the sample or model as fully as he desired or has refused to examine the goods there is no implied warranty with regard to defects which an examination ought in the circumstances to have revealed to him. . . ." G.L. c. 106, section 2-316.

and wholesome? * * * [N]obody is claiming that the fish it-self wasn't wholesome. * * * But the bone of contention here—I don't mean that for a pun—but was this fish bone a foreign substance that made the fish chowder unwholesome or not fit to be eaten?"

The plaintiff has vigorously reminded us of the high stan-dards imposed by this court where the sale of food is involved (citation omitted) and has made reference to cases involving stones in beans (citation omitted), trichinae in pork (citation omitted), and to certain other cases here and elsewhere, serving to bolster her contention of breach of warranty.

The defendant asserts that here was a native New Englander eating fish chowder in a "quaint" Boston dining place where she had been before; that "[f]ish chowder as it is served and en-joyed by New Englanders, is a hearty dish, originally designed to satisfy the appetites of our seamen and fishermen"; that "[t]his court knows well that we are not talking of some insipid broth as is customarily served to convalescents." We are asked to rule in such fashion that no chef is forced "to reduce the pieces of fish in the chowder to miniscule size in an effort to ascertain if they contained any pieces of bone." "In so ruling," we are told (in the defendant's brief), "the court will not only uphold its reputation for legal knowledge and acumen, but will, as loyal sons of Massachusetts, save our world-renowned fish chowder from degenerating into an insipid broth containing the mere essence of its former stature as a culinary master-piece." Notwithstanding these passionate entreaties, we are bound to examine with detachment the nature of fish chowder and what might happen to it under varying interpretations of the Uniform Commercial Code.

Chowder is an ancient dish preexisting even "the appetites of our seamen and fishermen." It was perhaps the common an-cestor of the "more refined cream soups, purees, and bisques." Berolzheimer, The American Woman's Cook Book (Publisher's

Guild Inc., New York, 1941) p. 176. The word "chowder" comes from the French "chaudière," meaning a "cauldron" or "pot." "In the fishing villages of Brittany * * * 'faire la chaudière' means to supply a cauldron in which is cooked a mess of fish and biscuit with some savoury condiments, a hodge-podge contributed by the fishermen themselves, each of whom in turn receives his share of the prepared dish. The Breton fishermen probably carried the custom to Newfoundland, long famous for its chowder, whence it has spread to Nova Scotia, New Brunswick, and New England." A New English Dictionary (MacMillan and Co., 1893) p. 386. Our literature over the years abounds in references not only to the delights of chowder but also to its manufacture. A namesake of the plaintiff, Daniel Webster, had a recipe for fish chowder which has survived into a number of modern cookbooks[2] and in which the removal of fish bones is not mentioned at all. One old time recipe recited in the New England Dictionary study defines chowder as "A dish made of fresh fish (esp. cod) or clams, stewed with pieces of pork or bacon, onions, and biscuit. 'Cider and champagne are sometimes added.'" Hawthorne, in the House of the Seven Gables (Allyn and Bacon, Boston, 1957) p. 8, speaks of "[a] codfish of sixty pounds, caught in the bay, [which] had been dissolved into the rich liquid of a chowder."

---

2. "Take a cod of ten pounds, well cleaned, leaving on the skin. Cut into pieces one and a half pounds thick, preserving the head whole. Take one and a half pounds of clear, fat salt pork, cut into thin slices. Do the same with twelve potatoes. * * * Try out the pork first, then take out the pieces of pork, leaving in the drippings. Add to that three parts of water, a layer of fish, so as to cover the bottom of the pot; next a layer of potatoes, then two tablespoons of salt, 1 teaspoon of pepper, then the pork, another layer of fish, and the remainder of the potatoes. Fill the pot with water to cover the ingredients. Let the chowder boil twenty-five minutes. When this is done have a quart of boiling milk ready, and ten hard crackers split and dipped in cold water. Add milk and crackers. Let the whole boil five minutes. The chowder is then ready to be first-rate if you have followed the directions." Wolcott, The Yankee Cook Book (Coward-McCann, Inc., New York City, 1939) p. 9.

A chowder variant, cod "Muddle," was made in Plymouth in the 1890s by taking "a three or four pound codfish, head added. Season with salt and pepper and boil in just enough water to keep from burning. When cooked, add milk and piece of butter."[3] The recitation of these ancient formulae suffices to indicate that in the construction of chowders in these parts in other years, worries about fish bones played no role whatsoever. This broad outlook on chowders has persisted in more modern cookbooks. "The chowder of today is much the same as the old chowder * * *." The American Woman's Cook Book, supra, p. 176. The all embracing Fannie Farmer states in a portion of her recipe, fish chowder is made with a "fish skinned, but head and tail left on. Cut off head and tail and remove fish from backbone. Cut fish into 2-inch pieces and set aside. Put head, tail, and backbone broken in pieces, in stewpan; add 2 cups cold water and bring slowly to boiling point * * *." The liquor thus produced from the bones is added to the balance of the chowder. Farmer, The Boston Cooking School Cook Book (Little Brown Co., 1937) p. 166.

Thus we consider a dish which for many long years, if well made, has been made generally as outlined above. It is not too much to say that a person sitting down in New England to consume a good New England fish chowder embarks on a gustatory adventure which may entail the removal of some fish bones from his bowl as he proceeds. We are not inclined to tamper with age old recipes by any amendment reflecting the plaintiff's view of the effect of the Uniform Commercial Code upon them. We are aware of the heavy body of case law involving foreign substances in food, but we sense a strong distinction between them and those relative to unwholesomeness of the food itself, e.g., tainted mackerel (citation omitted) and a fish bone in a fish chowder. Certain Massachusetts cooks might

---

3. Atwood, Receipts for Cooking Fish (Avery & Doten, Plymouth 1896) p. 8.

cavil at the ingredients contained in the chowder in this case in that it lacked the heartening lift of salt pork. In any event, we consider that the joys of life in New England include the ready availability of fresh fish chowder. We should be prepared to cope with the hazards of fish bones, the occasional presence of which in chowder is, it seems to us, to be anticipated, and which, in the light of a hallowed tradition, do not impair their fitness or merchantability. While we are buoyed in this conclusion by Shapiro v. Hotel Statler Corp., 132 F.Supp. 891 (S.D.Cal.), in which the bone which afflicted the plaintiff appeared in "Hot Barquette of Seafood Mornay," we know that the United States District Court of Southern California, situated as are we upon a coast, might be expected to share our views. We are most impressed, however, by Allen v. Grafton, 170 Ohio St. 249, 164 N.E.2d 167, where in Ohio, the Midwest, in a case where the plaintiff was injured by a piece of oyster shell in an order of fried oysters, Mr. Justice Taft (now Chief Justice) in a majority opinion held that "the possible presence of a piece of oyster shell in or attached to an oyster is so well known to anyone who eats oysters that we can say as a matter of law that one who eats oysters can reasonably anticipate and guard against eating such a piece of shell   *   *   * ." (P. 259 of 170 Ohio St., p. 174 of 164 N.Ed.2d.)

Thus, while we sympathize with the plaintiff who has suffered a peculiarly New England injury, the order must be

Exceptions sustained.

Judgment for the defendant.

Advising Margaret Fox

After reading *Webster*, Mr. Palmer reflected on his situation. Unfortunately the court in *Webster* did not state whether it reached its decision based on the foreign/natural test, the reasonable expectation test or just some ad hoc analysis of what is unmerchantable. However, he thought of arguments for why The Fearless Flounder should be liable. He called Margaret Fox to give her his advice.

"Margaret, I've got some good news and some bad news," he began. "The good news is that there is a Massachusetts law that makes restaurants responsible for any harm their customers suffer if they serve them bad food. The law requires that the party serving the food is a merchant and that the customer has bought the food. That means that if friends of yours got salmonella poisoning from turkey you served them at a dinner party, they couldn't sue you under this law because you are not a merchant and they hadn't paid for their food.

"That's a relief," said Margaret, a bit sarcastically. "Go on, Nelson."

"OK. The problem for us is the third requirement that the food must be unmerchantable."

"Why is that a problem?" Margaret cried. "That bone wasn't supposed to be there. It scraped my throat and I had to go to the hospital. That fish shouldn't have been sold with a bone in it!"

"I know it sounds strange to you, but we have a rather unusual legal situation here. This same law is part of almost every state's statutes. However, since the law applies to things other than food, the definitions for what makes something merchantable don't really fit food. The courts in each state have had to decide what merchantable means.

Some states have what is known as the foreign/natural test for merchantability. If the substance that caused the injury was natural to the food, the food is merchantable. Other states use what is known as the reasonable expectation test. If a person would reasonably expect the substance that caused the injury to be in the food, that person could guard against any harm it might cause, and the food would be considered merchantable."

"Well, don't keep me in suspense. What test does Massachusetts use?" asked Margaret.

"I wish I could tell you. That's what makes this unusual. The last Massachusetts case to address the issue, *Webster v. Blue Ship Tea Room,* was decided decades ago, and its wording was very ambiguous. One of the sentences in the opinion suggests the *Webster* court used the foreign/natural test. '[W]as this fish bone a foreign substance that made the fish chowder unwholesome or not fit to be eaten?'"

"That doesn't sound too encouraging to me," said Margaret. "It was a fishbone in fish that hurt me."

"Well, there is a slightly more encouraging sentence in the opinion. 'We should be prepared to cope with the hazard of fish bones, the occasional presence of which in chowders is, it seems to us to be anticipated, and which in the light of a hallowed tradition, do not impair their fitness or merchantability.'"

"Why is that encouraging? Didn't the person who ate the chowder with the bone lose?"

"That's true, but that sentence might mean that there had been a discussion of what the customer should have anticipated before making that decision. I think we have an argument in your case that even if someone would have anticipated a bone in fish chowder, no one would expect a bone in a piece of haddock filet. *Webster* is full of fish chowder recipes, and the opinion makes the point that no fish chowder recipe calls for the removal of bones. Therefore, no customer should expect fish chowder to be free of bones, and finding a bone did not make the chowder unmerchantable.

However, you ate filet of haddock with lobster sauce. The word 'filet' means boneless. Customers who order 'filets' do not anticipate bones in their fish and would not take any precaution against being injured. I think we have an argument that your fish filet was unmerchantable."

Margaret sounded happier, "I like that argument."

"I thought you would. There is another possibility for how the *Webster* court came to its decision. It might have used neither of the two established tests. Instead it might have come to its conclusion by some ad hoc analysis of what makes food merchantable or unmerchantable. The court might have intended that each case should get decided on its own merits. The *Webster* court might have intended to make clear that fish chowder with a bone in it is merchantable, but it did not intend to imply anything about other situations like fish bones in fish filet.

"Give me the bottom line. What will happen if I decide to sue The Fearless Flounder?"

Mr. Palmer was honest about her chances. "A lot depends on the initial judge. If he or she believes that the *Webster* court used the foreign/natural test, your case will be dismissed. Of course, you can then appeal the decision. The *Webster* case is old and the trend in other states is towards using the reasonable expectation test. You might win on appeal. However, you would have spent much money and time on this matter.

If the initial judge believes that *Webster* was a reasonable expectation case (or one in which the court used an ad hoc analysis), your case will proceed. Then your success would be a matter of how convincingly I can demonstrate that it is not reasonable to expect a fish bone in fish filet."

Margaret Fox thought about it for a few minutes, then said, "I want to go ahead."

Drafting the Complaint

Mr. Palmer then wrote a document called a complaint, which he sent to The Fearless Flounder. It notified the restaurant that it was being sued.

COMMONWEALTH OF MASSACHUSETTS

SUFFOLK, SS   SUPERIOR COURT
                                        CIVIL ACTION NO.

MARGARET FOX
    Plaintiff

    v.

THE FEARLESS FLOUNDER
    Defendant

COMPLAINT

1. The plaintiff is a resident of Boston, County of Suffolk.

2. The defendant is a Massachusetts corporation with a usual place of business in Boston, County of Suffolk.

3. The defendant is engaged in the operation of a restaurant.

4. An order of filet of haddock with lobster sauce was purchased by the plaintiff from the defendant.

5. The plaintiff relied upon the defendant's warranty that the fish was fit for human consumption and was free from all injurious substances. However, the fish contained an injurious substance.

6. Notice of the breach of warranty was duly given to the defendant.

7. As a result of eating the fish, the plaintiff was injured by a fish bone in the dinner and was obliged to expend money for medical care, and was otherwise damaged.

Whereas the plaintiff demands judgment against the defendant for damages and costs.

Nelson Palmer, Esq.
Attorney for Plaintiff[3]

---

3. Although the complaint does not list the elements of the implied warranty of merchantability, it does allege the facts that would satisfy all the elements. For example, stating that the defendant operates a restaurant in item 3 of the complaint is important to show that the defendant is a merchant. The use of the word "purchase" in item 4 shows that there was a sale. The statement that the food contained "an injurious substance" shows that there was a breach of the warranty any restaurant gives its customers.

Advising The Fearless Flounder

The restaurant owner, Thomas Cain, got the complaint and called his lawyer, Doris Becker. She also read the Uniform Commercial Code and *Webster*. Ms. Becker's duty was to counsel her client whether to litigate or settle. Since in *Webster* the Blue Ship Tea Room won, she read *Webster* looking for ways the restaurant's situation in *Webster* was similar to that of her client, The Fearless Flounder.

After reading *Webster*, she called Mr. Cain.

"I think you are pretty safe here, Tom. The plaintiff's legal theory is the implied warranty of merchantability. To prevail the plaintiff must..."

"You know I don't want the details, Doris. Just tell me what I should do."

"The law seems to be in your favor. The most recent Massachusetts case on point is one in which the restaurant was found not liable for injuries to a person who swallowed a bone that was in her fish chowder. The only problem might be that the fish you served was called 'filet' on the menu, but I think I can deal with that nicely. I don't think you should make any effort to settle. I'll prepare the documents for the next step and call you.

"I trust you, Doris. I'll talk to you soon."

The Stages of Trial and Bases of Appeal

Background for this Chapter

Trial Court

Most states have a three tier legal system with what is known as the "trial court" as the entry point. It is the trial judge's responsibility to determine what existing law applies to a case. It is usually a jury's responsibility to decide the facts of a case. If a cause of action requires that the reasonableness of an action be determined, this usually is a matter of fact decided by the jury.

Decisions about what law applies are made early in the litigation process when lawyers for both parties appear before a judge to argue about the applicability of legal theories. If the judge agrees that the law proposed by the plaintiff is applicable, a jury is empaneled.

The jury will listen to witnesses, decide what really happened, and determine whether what happened fits the requirements of the cause or causes of action being proposed by the plaintiff. In some cases there is no jury, and the judge performs these jury functions.

Appellate Court

The second tier court (appellate court) hears the routine appeals granted to losers as a matter of right by state statute.

However, the loser cannot just say, "I appeal." The appeal must be couched in very specific language. Our system gives special deference to the decisions about the facts during a trial. The loser cannot base its appeal on what was decided during the trial about the facts (with limited exceptions). In theory, the losing party must claim that the judge made an error.

Some appeals are based on the losing party's claim that the judge made an error in deciding that the case should be stopped before going to the jury (motion to dismiss, motion for judgment on the pleadings, motion for summary judgment, motion for judgment as a matter of law). Some appeals are based on the losing party's claim that the judge has made an error during the course of trial that allowed the jury to come to the wrong decision (admission or denial of evidence, jury instructions). In other instances the losing party claims that the judge made an error in not overturning the verdict of the jury (renewal of motion for judgment after trial) or in not granting a new trial.

The appellate court can decide that the trial judge did not make an error, and it will "affirm" the decision of the trial court. It can also decide that the trial judge did make an error and "reverse" the decision of the trial court. Appellate courts set precedent for subsequent cases brought to the trial courts and to themselves.

Court of Last Resort

Sometimes the highest state court hears a case. There may be several second tier courts in the state, and they may have decided similar cases applying different law. This may have happened because there had been no case in the area of law decided by the highest court in the past or because a case decided by the highest court was ambiguously decided, as was *Webster*. Therefore, the lower appellate courts have used whichever test they thought most appropriate. The highest court will take a case in order to stop the uncertainty in the system.

Often high courts are looking for cases by which they can overturn old existing precedent or make new law. Our system will not allow the court to do either on its own. It must wait for a case in order to rule on a particular issue. Sometimes the highest court will reach down into an intermediate appellate court and take a case in order to rule quickly on an issue it deems important.

Stages of Trial

The case of *Fox v. The Fearless Flounder* would have different outcomes depending on how the trial judge interprets *Webster*. This section presents the alternatives. The first three sections are complicated so do not worry if they are not clear to you immediately. The next two chapters should make them clearer.

Once Mr. Cain decided not to settle, Doris Becker had two possible next steps. She could have filed (1) a motion to dismiss or (2) an answer with the court. In both she would rely on the argument that if a harmful substance in food is natural to the food its presence does not render the food unmerchantable.

1. Motion to Dismiss[1]

Ms. Becker could file a legal defense in what is called a motion to dismiss. The substance of the motion could be as short as one sentence.

---

1. In many of your first semester cases you will see the term "demurrer." This is an old term for a motion substantially identical to the modern "motion to dismiss." California still uses this term.

The defendant moves to dismiss the action because the complaint fails to state a claim against defendant upon which relief can be granted in that the fish was merchantable as a matter of law because a fish bone is natural to fish.

She would also submit a brief in support of her motion. In it she would point to the foreign/natural wording in *Webster*, "[W]as this fish bone a foreign substance that made the fish chowder unwholesome or not fit to be eaten?" If the question meant that the court used the foreign/natural test, then Margaret Fox would have no law upon which to bring her case in Massachusetts. The fish would be considered merchantable as a matter of law since fish bones are natural to fish. One of the elements necessary for the implied warranty of merchantability to be a cause of action would not be present. Therefore, there would be no legal foundation for the claim.

Nelson Palmer, would write a brief in opposition to the motion. In it he would argue that the *Webster* court used the reasonable expectation test. He would point to the reasonable expectation language in the opinion; "We should be prepared to cope with the hazard of fish bones, the occasional presence of which in chowders is, it seems to us to be anticipated, and which, in the light of a hallowed tradition, do not impair their fitness or merchantability." He also would state that if the court had been using the foreign/natural test, the opinion would have been much shorter, and there would have been no reason for fish chowder recipes.

At this point the two lawyers would present their arguments to a judge. Since the meaning of "merchantability" is a question of law, not fact, there would be need only for a judge. If the case goes to trial, Margaret Fox would have to give evidence and prove that her allegations are true in order to prevail. However, at this stage she would be given the benefit of the doubt. Her case would end only if the judge believes that there would be no legal foundation for her claim even if all the facts she alleges are proven true.

Therefore, the judge would have to make the important decision as to which is the most likely test used in *Webster*, or more accurately, which test the current Supreme Judicial Court would use in interpreting *Webster*.

If the judge believes that the Supreme Judicial Court would apply the foreign/natural test, the motion to dismiss would be granted, and the Margaret Fox case would stop. However, Margaret Fox could appeal the decision. If the appellate court disagreed with the judge's interpretation of the law, the decision would be reversed, and the trial would go forward.

If the judge believes that the Supreme Judicial Court would apply the reasonable expectation test, the motion to dismiss would not be granted. The trial would go forward.

Even in states in which the highest court has clearly stated that the foreign/natural test is the law, cases like the Fox case are brought if lawyer and client are convinced that a change in the law is possible. Perhaps the precedent is old and/or recent cases in closely related areas of the law suggest a more consumer oriented approach. In food cases, trial judges grant motions to dismiss when the existing precedent is a case that espouses the foreign/natural test. The trial judge has no choice. Lower court judges must follow the precedent set by prior appellate cases. However, when this case is appealed, the higher court may decide that it is about time to change the law, and the ruling of the trial judge is overturned. The plaintiff has won the appeal from the granting of the motion to dismiss.

When you read appeals from the granting of a motion to dismiss, you must be careful not to read too much into the case. If the appellate court overturns the decision of the trial court to grant a motion to dismiss, it does not mean that the plaintiff has won the case. All that has been "won" is the right for the plaintiff to go forward to trial. You know what law is going to be applied in the case, but you do not know the outcome.

Many students are frustrated when they realize that they will not know the eventual outcome of the case they have read. However, the outcome is important only to the parties in the case. Since no two cases are exactly alike, it would be irrelevant to practicing lawyers and law students to know what one jury decided on one day about one very particular set of facts.

2. Answer

Instead of a motion to dismiss, Ms. Becker could file an answer to the complaint with the court in which she would state as a defense the insufficiency of the claim. In other words, the requirements of the implied warranty of merchantibility are not met because the food was merchantable.

COMMONWEALTH OF MASSACHUSETTS

SUFFOLK, SS   SUPERIOR COURT
                                 CIVIL ACTION NO.

MARGARET FOX
    Plaintiff

   v.

THE FEARLESS FLOUNDER
    Defendant

ANSWER

1. The defendant has no knowledge of the allegations in paragraph one of the complaint.

2. The defendant admits the allegations in paragraph two of the complaint.

3. The defendant admits the allegations in paragraph three of the complaint.

4. The defendant admits the allegations in paragraph four of the complaint.

5. The defendant denies the allegations in paragraph five of the complaint.

6. The defendant admits that the plaintiff informed the defendant that she had been injured as alleged in paragraph six of the complaint.

7. The defendant has no knowledge of the allegations in paragraph seven of the complaint

Defense

The complaint fails to state a claim against the defendant on which relief can be granted.

3. Motion for Judgment on the Pleadings

After the defendant submits an answer to the complaint, either side can file a motion for judgment on the pleadings. If the motion is granted, the party making the motion wins.

If Doris Becker filed a motion to dismiss

If the judge in the Margaret Fox case believes that the law in Massachusetts is "reasonable expectation," the motion to dismiss filed by Doris Becker would not be granted. Now she must file an answer. She could state in her answer a factual defense, if true. The following warning might have appeared on all menus of The Fearless Flounder: "Be aware that all fish have bones, and we cannot guarantee that your meal is boneless. Please use every caution when you eat your fish to avoid injury."

Then Ms. Becker would file a motion for judgment on the pleadings. The judge might believe that with this warning, a customer would reasonably expect to find a bone in the fish and guard against swallowing one. Even if Margaret Fox could prove at trial that all three elements of the implied warranty of merchantability had been present, The Fearless Flounder would not be liable because the warning was all that was necessary. The case would stop, but Margaret Fox could use the granting of the motion as the basis of her appeal.

If Doris Becker filed an answer only

After filing her answer, Doris Becker could file a motion for judgment on the pleadings. If the trial judge believes that Massachusetts is a foreign/natural state, the motion would be granted. The case would stop, but Margaret Fox could use the granting of the motion as the basis of her appeal.

4. Motion for summary judgment

If the plaintiff's case survives a motion to dismiss and a motion for judgment on the pleadings, or neither motion was filed, the next point at which the litigation may be stopped is after what is known as "discovery." Among other things, discovery involves taking depositions and obtaining affidavits from parties and experts. If the judge believes that discovery has revealed that there are no facts in dispute, then a motion for summary judgment can be granted. The language you will read in your cases is, "[T]here is no genuine issue as to any material fact and the moving party is entitled to a judgment as a matter of law."

Both parties can file motions for summary judgment. If the plaintiff files the motion and it is granted, the case is stopped and the plaintiff wins. If the defendant files the motion and it is granted, the case is stopped and the defendant wins. If neither side's motion for summary judgment is granted, it means that the judge believes that there is a "genuine issue of material fact," so the case must proceed and be presented to the jury.

Margaret Fox's Motion for Summary Judgment

Margaret Fox would get to the summary judgment stage only if the judge believes that *Webster* was a reasonable expectation case and, therefore, does not grant The Fearless Flounder's motion to dismiss. If Margaret Fox files a motion for summary judgment and the judge grants it, she would win. To decide whether to grant Margaret Fox's motion, the judge needs to decide if the presence of this particular bone in the fish filet was so unreasonable that the case need not be sent to the jury (no "genuine issue of material fact").

The judge might grant the motion if he or she believes that no consumer would expect a bone (1) in a dish called filet, especially when (2) that filet is covered by sauce.

We have seen that what is reasonable is usually something that is a matter of fact to be decided by the jury. "Reasonableness" is considered a matter of law and decided by the judge only if the judge believes that no jury could decide otherwise. If Margaret Fox's motion for summary judgment is not granted, the trial will proceed so the jury can decide whether it is reasonable or unreasonable to find the bone.

The Fearless Flounder's Motion for Summary Judgment

If The Fearless Flounder files a motion for summary judgment, it will be granted if the judge believes that the presence of the fish bone in a filet of fish with lobster sauce is so reasonable that the case need not be sent to the jury to decide. If the motion is granted, Margaret Fox can appeal this decision. If the appeals court reverses the trial judge, what she wins is the right to go forward to trial. The effect of the appeals court reversing the granting of the motion for summary judgment by the trial court is the same as the effect of it reversing the granting of the motion to dismiss.

When a Motion to Dismiss Becomes a Motion for Summary Judgment

If a judge in reviewing a motion to dismiss looks at anything other than the complaint, the motion becomes one for summary judgment. Some cases you will read began with a motion to dismiss filed by the defendant. However, for some reason the judge could not make a decision based on the complaint only. Deposition information or expert witness documents might be needed. When the judge finally decides, the decision is deemed to be a response to a motion for summary judgment.

Margaret Fox's complaint stated that the bone was a fish bone. However, if it had been unclear just what kind of bone it was, Margaret Fox's complaint might have alleged merely that there was a bone in the filet of fish. Ms. Becker might have filed a motion to dismiss assuming the bone was a fish bone. Regardless of whether the judge believed that *Webster* was a foreign/natural or reasonable expectation case, he or she would need to know what kind of bone it was. The judge would await an affidavit from an expert about the bone. Even in reasonable expectation states foreign substances are considered unmerchantable as a matter of law, so if the bone turned out to be a chicken bone or a piece of clam shell, Margaret Fox would prevail.

If the judge believes that *Webster* was a foreign/natural case, the motion of The Fearless Flounder would be granted once it is determined the bone is a fish bone. However, although it was filed as a motion to dismiss, the order would state that it is a granting of a motion for summary judgment since something other than the complaint was reviewed.

Many of the cases in this book seem only to be about which test should be used, the foreign/natural or the reasonable expectation. Therefore, they seem like motion to dismiss cases. However, if you read closely you will see that the judge may have read depositions or affidavits. *Yong Cha Hong* in the next chapter is one of these cases.

5. Evidence

The basis of appeal most familiar to the lay person is the improper admission of evidence or the improper denial of admission of evidence. We know about this from TV dramas when the lawyers often stand up and say, "Objection, your honor." This means that the lawyer believes that the judge is not correctly applying the rules of evidence. After the trial is over, the losing party may appeal the jury verdict if the lawyer has objected to the admission of evidence or the denial of the admission of evidence during the trial. If the appellate court agrees that the judge made an error in applying the rules of evidence, it can grant the losing party a new trial. However, this happens only if the appellate court also agrees that the error actually made a difference in the verdict. If it believes that verdict would have been the same, the appeal will be denied. You may not read any evidence cases in your first year classes because casebook editors know that you probably will take a whole course on the rules of evidence later in your law school career.

6. Motion for judgment as a matter of law (formerly "motion for a directed verdict")

There is one more stage at which the judge may stop the case before a verdict is reached by the jury. After the jury has heard the evidence of one party, the other party can file a motion for judgment as a matter of law. The party is saying that the evidence presented by its opponent is so weak that there is no reason for this case to go the jury. After the opposing party has presented its evidence (all evidence is in), either party can file the motion. Each party is saying that its case is so strong that "reasonable men could not differ" about the result. If the judge agrees with one of the parties, the motion of that party would be granted. This means that the jury does not deliberate about the case, and the party whose motion is granted wins the case.

It is not common for judges to grant motions for judgment as a matter of law. There is very little to gain and much to lose. The major work of the trial has been done. There are few court costs to be saved. In addition, the judge runs the risk of being reversed on appeal. It's much safer to let the jury make the decision.

Although rarely granted, motions for judgment as a matter of law are routinely filed by both parties in a case. This is because in most jurisdictions a party cannot file one of the post verdict motions if it did not file a motion for judgment as a matter of law. The lawyers' bills are mounting.

If the judge does grant one party's motion, the losing party can appeal. The appeal would state that the judge made an error in granting the motion. If the judge grants neither side's motion, the case just continues to a verdict. At the conclusion of the trial, the losing side can appeal stating that the judge made an error in not granting that side's motion for judgment as a matter of law.

7. Instructions to the Jury

Any party may (but is not required to) file written requests that the court instruct the jury on the law as that party interprets it. Copies of requests must be furnished to the opposing parties. This may occur at the close of the evidence or earlier, as the judge directs. If the jury instructions of the party which eventually loses the case were not given by the judge, that party can use that fact as a basis of appeal for the case. The argument would be that the judge gave the wrong instructions. The jury would have not decided the way it did if the right instructions had been given.

"Instructions should instruct the jury as to their duty to apply the law given by the court to the facts proven by the evidence, to weigh the evidence and to judge the credibility of testimony, to resolve conflicts in the evidence whenever possible, to view the instructions as a whole applying them to all the evidence admitted at the trial, and their duty to base their decision upon a consideration of all of the evidence in the case." *Kelley v. Stop & Shop*, 530 N.E.2d 190 (1988)

The jury instructions for the Margaret Fox case might be something like, "If you find that a fish bone is not reasonably to be expected in a dish called filet of fish, then you will find the food unmerchantable."

If the sufficiency of the jury instructions is the issue raised on appeal, the appeals court decides whether the instructions were (1) erroneous, and (2) whether they were so erroneous that the case should be retried before a properly instructed jury. If the instructions were erroneous, but not sufficiently so as to have misled the jury, the appeal is not granted.

8. Renewal of motion for judgment after trial (formerly "motion for judgment notwithstanding the verdict" — JNOV)

A renewal of motion for judgment after trial is made after a verdict is announced. As the name of the motion suggests, it is considered only a renewal of a previous motion and cannot be made if the motion for judgment as a matter of law was not made. The losing party is essentially saying in its motion, "Judge, you really thought our evidence was the strongest. You wanted to grant our motion earlier. Now you have a chance to do the right thing and decide in our favor. You will give judgment for us notwithstanding the verdict of the jury." If the trial judge denies the motion, this denial is cited as the error the judge made in the losing party's appeal.

9. Motion for new trial

There are a variety of reasons used by losing parties in requesting a new trial. There may have been prejudicial misconduct by the jury, lawyer for the opposing side, or judge. For example, if a jury considers something other than evidence admitted at trial, that is grounds for a new trial. If the jury in the Margaret Fox case had decided to go to dinner at The Fearless Flounder and order filet with lobster sauce, their experience might be considered evidence not admitted at trial and warrant a new trial. Sometimes new evidence is discovered, and the losing party files the motion with the trial judge.

If the trial judge denies the motion, the losing party can file an appeal stating that the judge made an error in not granting the new trial.

Importance of this Chapter to First Year Law Students

Most cases you will read in law school are appellate cases, and usually the opinion will specify the particular error the losing party claims that the judge made. The error is often called the "procedural" issue in a case to distinguish it from the "substantive" issue. For example, in *Webster* one of the procedural issues cited in the case (omitted from the text in the first chapter) is the refusal of the judge "to direct a verdict for the defendant." The substantive issue, and the reason you read the case, is the meaning of "merchantable." Students who do not know this distinction are confused by the language in a case which might read something like, "The only issue before us is whether the judge erred in directing the verdict for defendant."

Procedural issues are usually of secondary importance in most of your courses. However, if you do not have a basic knowledge of them, your reading of cases will be slow. This chapter has provided an overview of the common procedural issues so that you will read cases efficiently early in the semester. The terminology used is that of the recently revised Federal Rules of Civil Procedure. However, most of the cases you will read in your courses will have been decided before the revision, so the old terms are given as well.

Cases

Components

Unfortunately for us there is no one format required for a legal opinion. The most we can do is realize that there usually are certain topics that appear in a case somewhere.

1. The legal theory or theories under which the case has been begun

Although you might expect judges to explicitly state the applicable cause of action at the beginning of every case, this rarely happens. If you look for the rule in the cases I use in this book, you will find it sometimes buried in the body of the case, in a footnote, or it may not be stated at all. Lawyers will know the plaintiff's cause of action before they even start to read the case. Mr. Palmer knew what Mrs. Webster's legal theory was because he found *Webster* by looking up references to the implied warranty of merchantability mentioned in the Massachusetts statute book.

Since judges sometimes are lax about making the cause of action explicit, many students cannot tell me the plaintiff's cause or causes of action in a case we are discussing. You need a method of determining what the cause of action is in a case before you start reading it so you don't waste time trying to find it. Sometimes you can identify the cause of action before you read the case either from your course syllabus or from the table of contents in your casebook. Sometimes you will need to turn to legal textbooks called "hornbooks" or other study materials.

2. The element of the cause of action at issue in the case

In the Margaret Fox complaint there were allegations that, if proven, would result in the Fearless Flounder being liable. The implied warranty of merchantability requires that there be (1) a merchant, (2) a sale, and (3) unmerchantable food. In most of the cases you will read (like the Margaret Fox case), the defendant cannot argue that it was not a merchant and that there was no sale. Therefore, at an early stage the defendant will concede that these elements are clearly present. Often this happens in the answer the defendant must submit in response to the plaintiff's complaint. Therefore, before the judge responds to the first motion, only one or possibly two of the elements are still at issue. The others are never mentioned in the opinion. You can see this in the *Webster* case. There is no mention of the elements of sale and merchant.

Not mentioning all the elements of the cause of action is no problem for the lawyer who reads the case looking only for the element at issue. The lawyer, like Mr. Palmer, has already looked up the law and is focused on the element of merchantability. You are at a disadvantage because you are using the cases to learn the law. Without a mention of all of the elements of the cause of action, you cannot reinforce your knowledge of them. You must keep in mind that the cases you read are chosen for their suitability for making you think about one of the elements. Your casebook may not make explicit the elements of a cause of action, but usually it will contain at least one case in which each element of a cause of action is at issue. You can consult a hornbook or study aid to find the rules and elements. This will help you determine which element is at issue in any one case when you read it. In implied warranty of merchantability cases, you know the case must be about either the element of merchant, sale, or the merchantability of the goods. The text of the case should make it clear which one is at issue.

3. Facts in the dispute

Some cases have long statements of the facts, some contain few facts. In implied warranty of merchantability cases, the cases with few facts are usually those in which the purpose of the case is to give a state court of last resort the opportunity to settle the question of whether the test to be applied in that state to the element of merchantability is foreign/natural or reasonable expectation. The only fact that is important to these cases is the naturalness of the offending substance. These are the motion to dismiss or motion for summary judgment cases. Other motion to dismiss or summary judgment cases have long fact statements, but there are no good legal reasons for such length. A motion to dismiss case with a long fact statement may mean the judge was intrigued by the case or the judge just may be especially long winded.

Most cases with long fact statements are those which are directed verdict or JNOV cases. Here both sides have presented evidence, and now the facts become important. For example, the *Webster* case is an appeal from the trial judge's refusal to grant a directed verdict or a JNOV ("motion for the entry of a verdict in its favor"). Both sides presented information that the court can now use. Much of the case is a restatement of plaintiff's and defendant's presentation of evidence at trial.

Facts are now important because the court is being asked to rule on whether the trial judge made an error in not reversing a decision of the jury. In *Webster* Mrs. Webster won on the trial level. The jury believed that the food was unmerchantable. However, the Supreme Judicial Court believed the trial judge erred in not granting the defendant's JNOV. Therefore it needed to present the facts that buttress its position that fish chowder which contains a fish bone is merchantable. Thus, there are fish chowder recipes and long discussions of just how "hearty" fish chowder is supposed to be.

4. Procedural History of the Case

The procedural history is very important to lawyers in the jurisdiction in which the case was decided. They must know whether a case is one decided by the court of last resort and must be dealt with as a possible precedent case, or is one decided by an intermediate appellate court and, therefore, has limited value as precedent. Usually the procedural history is of no practical use to you since you do not have a client in that jurisdiction.

Be prepared for the fact that the names of the various levels of courts are not the same in all states. The Supreme Court in one state may be the highest court, in another it may be the trial court. The names of the courts usually are irrelevant in your substantive courses.

5. The Basis for the Appeal

The importance of any appellate case for a lawyer is partially determined by where in the course of the case the appeal was taken. If a precedent case is a reversal of the trial judge's use of the foreign/natural test in the granting of a motion for summary judgment or a motion to dismiss, all the lawyer knows is that the law in that state is reasonable expectation. The lawyer knows nothing about what happened when that case was tried before a jury. A cherry pit in cherry pecan ice cream might be found to be reasonably expected or it may not. Even if a lawyer had a case in which a cherry pit in cherry pecan ice cream caused the injury, there would be no way for that lawyer to predict the outcome.

However, if a precedent case reverses a trial judge's refusal to grant a JNOV, then the lawyer knows whether it is or isn't reasonable to find a cherry pit in cherry pecan ice cream. Although a lawyer might find some differences between his case and the precedent case (peach pecan ice cream), counseling a client in this situation about bringing a case is very different from counseling when the precedent is a motion to dismiss case.

Since you are not serving a client, these distinctions are not important to you. However, you will better understand and appreciate how our legal system works if you know just how much weight can be placed on a case you read.

4. The Court's Decision and Its Reasoning

The most important aspect of a case for you is the court's reasons for what it decided. Since you are not representing a client in the jurisdiction of that case, you cannot use any of its procedural information. What you must learn is the kind of argument a lawyer makes about the elements of a cause of action. Therefore, what you must concentrate on is why the court decided the way it did. Did the court rely on our changing eating habits to decide? Did it cite the way this particular food is prepared? It might mention that what one might reasonably expect and be expected to guard against is different if the offending substance is a pearl in raw oysters or a pearl in a can of oysters. You learn to make arguments that will be useful to your future clients eventually and to you on your exams now.

Sample Cases

Following are three cases which illustrate some of the important concepts in the cases you will read in law school. You will want to reread the cases after reading the explanatory material that follows them.

Yong Cha Hong v. Marriott Corporation (1987)

Yong Cha Hong is one of my favorite cases. It is entertaining but also very instructive about our legal system. This is a trial court opinion written by a federal judge in the United States District Court in the District of Maryland. The judge denied defendant's motion for summary judgment.

The facts are simple. Yong Cha Hong was eating a wing of Roy Rogers fried chicken when she bit down on something she thought was a worm. She sued the Marriott Corporation (parent of Roy Rogers) for $500,000.00 because of the "great physical and emotional upset from her encounter with this item, including permanent injuries."

There are several words used in the opinion you should know before you read it.

> prays—request contained in a complaint which asks for the relief (remedy) to which the plaintiff thinks himself entitled
>
> count—a distinct statement of a plaintiff's cause of action
>
> deposition—a method of pretrial discovery of evidence which consists of a statement of a witness under oath, taken in question and answer form as it would be in court, with opportunity given to the adversary to be present and cross-examine, with all this reported and transcribed stenographically

judicial notice — court takes note of certain facts which are such common knowledge that there would be no need for a party to give evidence to prove them

Yong Cha Hong v. Marriott Corporation
United States District Court, District of Maryland, 1987
656 F. Supp. 445

SMALKIN, District Judge.

The plaintiff, Yong Cha Hong, commenced this case in a Maryland court with a complaint alleging counts of negligence and breach of warranty against defendants, the proprietor of a chain of fast food restaurants called Roy Rogers Family Restaurants (Marriott) and the supplier of raw frying chicken to the chain (Gold Kist). The case was removed to this Court on diversity grounds. It seems that the plaintiff was contentedly munching away one day on a piece of Roy Rogers take-out fried chicken[1] (a wing) when she bit into something in the chicken that she perceived to be a worm. She suffered, it is alleged, great physical and emotional upset from her encounter with this item, including permanent injuries, in consequence of which she prays damages in the amount of $500,000.00.

The defendants moved for summary judgment on plaintiff's warranty count, and also, later, as to the entire complaint, on the ground that there is no genuine dispute of material fact and that, as a matter of law, there was no breach of warranty or negligence. If they are right, they are entitled to summary judgment. (citations omitted).

It appears that the item encountered by plaintiff in the chicken wing was probably not a worm or other parasite, *see*

---

1. The Court takes judicial notice (because it is so well known in this jurisdiction) that Roy Rogers specializes in fried chicken, to eat in or take out....

Strasburger & Siegel Certificate of Analysis (Partial S.J. Motion Ex. A), although plaintiff, in her deposition, steadfastly maintains that it was a worm, notwithstanding the expert analysis. If it was not in fact a worm, *i.e.*, if the expert analysis is correct, it was either one of the chicken's major blood vessels (the aorta) or its trachea, both of which (the Court can judicially notice) would appear worm-like (although not meaty like a worm, but hollow) to a person unschooled in chicken anatomy. The Court must presume plaintiff to be inexpert as to chickens, even though she admits to some acquaintance with fresh-slaughtered chickens. (citation omitted). For the purposes of analyzing the plaintiff's warranty claim, the Court will assume that the item was not a worm. Precisely how the aorta or trachea wound up in this hapless chicken's wing is a fascinating, but as yet unanswered (and presently immaterial), question.

Thus, the warranty issue squarely framed is, does Maryland law[2] provide a breach of warranty[3] remedy for personal injury flowing from an unexpected encounter with an inedible[4] part of the chicken's anatomy in a piece of fast food fried chicken? Defendants contend that there can be no warranty recovery unless the offending item was a "foreign object," *i.e.*, not a part of the chicken itself.

In *Webster v. Blue Ship Tea Room, Inc.*, 347 Mass. 421, 198 N.E.2d 309 (1964), a favorite of commercial law teachers,[5] the plaintiff was injured when a fish bone she encountered in a

---

2. Of course, Maryland law applies in this diversity case. *Erie Railroad v. Tompkins*, 304 U.S. 64, 58 S.Ct. 817, 82 L.Ed. 1188 (1938).

3. The relevant warranty is found in *Md. Comm. Law Code Ann.* [U.C.C.] §2-314(2) (1975). The Maryland U.C.C. warranty of merchantability applies to sales of food in restaurants, including take-out sales. U.C.C. §2-314 (1).

4. Although perhaps digestible the aorta and the trachea of a chicken would appear indisputably to belong to the realm of the inedible in that fowl's anatomy.

5. Of which this Judge is one (part time).

bowl of New England fish chowder, served in a "quaint" Boston restaurant, became stuck in her throat. She was denied warranty recovery (on a theory of implied warranty of merchantability) on grounds that are not altogether clear from the court's opinion. The opinion can be read in several ways: (1) There was no breach because the bone was not extraneous, but a natural substance; (2) There was no breach because New England fish chowder always has bones as an unavoidable contaminant; or (3) The plaintiff, an undoubted Yankee, should have expected to find a bone in her chowder and should have slurped it more gingerly.

*   *   *

Unlike New England Fish Chowder, a well-known regional specialty, fried chicken (though of Southern origin) is a ubiquitous American dish. Chicken, generically, has a special place in the American poultry pantheon:

> The dream of the good life in America is embodied in the promise of "a chicken in every pot." Domestic and wild fowl have always been abundant and popular, and each wave of immigrants has brought along favorite dishes— such as paella and chicken cacciatore—which have soon become naturalized citizens.

The Fannie Farmer Cookbook (Knopf: 1980) at 228.

Indeed as to fried chicken, *Fannie Farmer* lists recipes for three varieties of fried chicken alone—pan-fried, batter-fried, and Maryland Fried chicken.[6] *Id.* at 238–39. As best this Judge can determine (and he is no culinary expert) the fast food chicken served in Roy Rogers most resembles Fannie Farmer's batter-fried chicken. That is, it is covered with a thick, crusty (often highly spiced) batter, that usually conceals from inspection

---

6. Oddly enough, Maryland Fried Chicken is seldom encountered in Maryland restaurants, though this judge has seen it on restaurant menus in Ireland and England.

whatever lurks beneath. There is deposition testimony from plaintiff establishing that she saw the offending item before she bit into it, having torn the wing asunder before eating it. A question of fact is raised as to just what she saw, or how carefully she might reasonably be expected to have examined what she saw before eating. It is common knowledge that chicken parts often harbor minor blood vessels. But this Judge, born and raised south of the Mason-Dixon Line (where fried chicken has been around longer than in any other part of America), knows of no special heightened awareness chargeable to fried chicken eaters that ought to caution them to be on the alert for tracheas or aortas in the middle of their wings.[7]

Certainly, in *Webster* and many other cases that have denied warranty recovery as a matter of law, the injurious substance was, as in this case, a natural (though inedible) part of the edible item consumed.... But in all these cases, the natural item was, beyond dispute, reasonably to be expected in the dish by its very nature, under the prevailing expectation of any reasonable consumer. Indeed, precisely this "reasonable expectation" test has been adopted in a number of cases (citations omitted). The "reasonable expectation" test has largely displaced the natural/foreign test adverted to by defendants. In the circumstances of this case and many others, it is the only one that makes sense. In the absence of any Maryland decisional law, and in view of the expense and impracticality of certification of the question to the Court of Appeals of Maryland in this case, this Court must decide the issue by applying the rule that that Court would likely adopt some time in the future. (citation omitted). This Court is confident that Maryland would apply

---

7. Of course, if as a matter of fact and law plaintiff abandoned her reliance on defendant's warranty by eating the wing with "contributory negligence," the defendants would have a good warranty defense, as well as a good negligence defense, under Maryland law. (citation omitted). But this is quintessentially a question of fact for the jury. (citation omitted).

the "reasonable expectation" rule to this warranty case, especially in view of the Court of Appeals' holding in *Bryer v. Rath Packing Co.,* 221 Md. 105, 156 A.2d 442 (1959), recognizing a negligence claim for the presence in a prepared food item of "something that should not be there" which renders the food unfit. *Id* at 112, 156 A.2d at 447.

Applying the reasonable expectation test to this case, the Court cannot conclude that the presence of a trachea or an aorta in a fast food fried chicken wing is so reasonably to be expected as to render it merchantable, as a matter of law, within the bounds of U.C.C. § 2-314(2). This is not like the situation involving a 1 cm. bone in a piece of fried fish in *Morrison's Cafeteria.* Everyone but a fool knows that tiny bones may remain in even the best filets of fish. This case is more like *Williams,* where the court held that the issue was for the trier of fact, on a claim arising from a cherry pit in cherry ice cream. Thus, a question of fact is presented that precludes the grant of summary judgment. (citation omitted). The jury must determine whether a piece of fast food fried chicken is merchantable if it contains an inedible item of the chicken's anatomy. Of course, the jury will be instructed that the consumer's reasonable expectations form a part of the merchantability concept (under the theory of ordinary fitness, U.C.C. § 2-314 (2)(c)), as do trade quality standards (under U.C.C. § 2-314 (2)(a)).

In short, summary judgment cannot be awarded defendants on plaintiff's warranty count, and their motion for partial summary judgment is, accordingly, *denied....*

Diversity Jurisdiction

Cases can be heard in federal court for one of two reasons. The first is the more obvious. Cases that involve federal questions such as those arising from the first amendment of the federal constitution are heard in federal court. There is at least one federal court in each state.

The second reason for a case to be heard in a federal court is under much scrutiny today because there is evidence that its reason for being no longer applies. Originally state court judges were considered less competent and more corruptible than federal court judges. When a plaintiff sued an out of state defendant in the plaintiff's state court, there was concern that the defendant could not be given a fair trial. Thus was born what is known as diversity jurisdiction. If the plaintiff and defendant are from different states and the amount in controversy is (currently) $75,000 or more, the case can be heard in the federal court. If the plaintiff brings the case in his or her state court, the defendant can have it "removed" to a federal court. You will learn the rules for removal in your Civil Procedure course.

In *Yong Cha Hong* the plaintiff was a citizen of Maryland, and she brought her case in a Maryland state court. It is not clear from the case in what state the defendant Marriott Corporation is considered to be a citizen. There are procedural rules which govern that question. However, it obviously must be a state other than Maryland, because the opinion states that "[t]he case was removed to this Court on diversity grounds." The amount in controversy requirement is satisfied because she claims damages ($500,000) in excess of the $50,000 requirement then applicable.

The Erie Doctrine

Once the case was in federal court, it became the judge's responsibility to determine what law to apply to the case. In the federal court, matters that are considered to be court procedure are governed by the Federal Rules of Civil Procedure. However, matters of substance are governed by state law. This may sound simple, but you will spend a great deal of time in your Civil Procedure course on the complications that can arise from what is called the Erie Doctrine.

The judge uses another set of rules to determine which of the two states' (Yong Cha Hong's home state or Marriott Corporation's home state) substantive law will apply. You may take a whole course about this subject, called Conflicts of Laws, but the specific rules are irrelevant here. What is important is that the judge determined that the conflicts rules required that Maryland law apply.

Once the proper state was determined, the judge was responsible for determining the Maryland law of the implied warranty of merchantability as it related to food. The most pressing question, obviously, was whether Maryland has adopted the foreign/natural or the reasonable expectation test. He found no precedent case to use ("absence of any Maryland decisional law"). He had two choices. He could have referred the question to the highest court in Maryland ("certifying" the question). This would ensure a certain answer, but essentially it would add an additional trial for both parties to endure. He took his other choice which was to "decide the issue by applying the rule that that Court would likely adopt some time in the future." In other words, our legal system allows a federal judge to decide what the law of a state would be.

In *Yong Cha Hong* Judge Smalkin decided that the Maryland Court of Appeals would apply the reasonable expectation test. He based his decision on the Maryland court's opinion in what he considered an analogous case. It is clear that he favors the reasonable expectation test. He states that it "has largely displaced the natural/foreign test adverted to by defendants," and he claims "it is the only one that makes sense." His decision has no precedent value within Maryland.

Summary Judgment

It is almost certain that there was no motion to dismiss filed by the defendant. There would be no point: the complaint would have stated a viable claim. There was a sale of food by a merchant, and the worm (a foreign substance) would make the food unmerchantable in every state. Therefore, the first chance for Marriott to get this case dismissed is after there is evidence obtained as to the real identity of the offending substance. The opinion references a certificate by an expert which stated that what Yong Cha Hong bit into was either a chicken trachea or aorta, and the judge based his judgment on his understanding that the substance was not a worm.

Now the defendant can file a motion for summary judgment. Evidently, Marriott filed the motion arguing in the alternative. Its first argument was that Maryland would apply the natural/foreign test. However, if the judge would determine that the Maryland court would apply the reasonable expectation test, then its second argument was that it was so reasonable to expect an aorta or trachea in a fried chicken wing that no jury would be needed to decide the issue. The judge could decide that it was reasonable as a matter of law and Marriott would win.

The judge decided that the test to be applied was the reasonable expectation test. He also decided that he could "not conclude that the presence of a trachea or an aorta in a fast food fried chicken wing is so reasonably to be expected as to render it merchantable as a matter of law." He would have granted the motion if the offending substance had been a 1 cm. bone in fish (*Morrison's*). In this case "[t]he jury must determine whether a piece of fast food fried chicken is merchantable if it contains an inedible item of the chicken's anatomy."

Yong Cha Hong has won the right to a trial. There is a "genuine issue of material fact." The issue of fact is whether it is reasonable to expect an aorta or trachea in a fried chicken wing.

Importance of the Case

This case is of no importance to lawyers as precedent. First of all it is a trial level decision. Secondly, it was decided in the federal court. Maryland lawyers cannot use it because it does not affect Maryland law. The importance of the case to lawyers is the same as it is to law students. It can provide arguments and ideas to be used in other cases. Lawyers may be in the position of arguing that a state's law should be the reasonable expectation test. They can use the judge's arguments for his preference. Both lawyers and law students can use the arguments the judge makes in justifying his denial of the motion for summary judgment. He cites the food preparation (Batter fried chicken is covered with a crust "that usually conceals from inspection whatever lurks beneath."). Should one be expected to search for offending substances? He notes the difference between this case and *Morrison's*, a case you will read later ("Everyone knows that tiny bones may remain in even the best filets of fish."). Your reading of the case should concentrate on the arguments you can use in other cases.

Reading the Case

Unless you knew what legal theory this case was about, you would not find it easily in the opinion. Look for the text of the implied warranty of merchantability in Footnote #3.

Williams v. Braum Ice Cream Stores, Inc. (1974)

Williams is a case decided by one of the appellate divisions of the court system of Oklahoma (a second tier appellate court). In this case Ms. Williams bought a "cherry pecan" ice cream cone from the defendant and broke a tooth on a cherry pit in the ice cream. The fact statement is quite short (as is the entire case) because the purpose of the case is to announce that the trial judge was wrong in granting the defendant's motion for summary judgment because the trial judge believed the correct standard for merchantability was foreign/natural.

This is a most unusual case in that it actually is a good teaching tool for law students because it contains a complete statement of the requirements of recovery under the implied warranty of merchantability. When you read the case, notice that the text of the warranty provision and the definition of merchantable are in the body of the opinion. It even explains that the defendant has agreed that it is a merchant. Most of the text of this short opinion is an explication of the two tests and the court's reasoning for choosing reasonable expectation.

Williams v. Braum Ice Cream Stores, Inc.
Oklahoma Court of Appeals, Division No. 1, 1974
534 P.2d 700

REYNOLDS, Judge:

Plaintiff-appellant brought this action against defendant-appellee for breach of implied warranty of merchantability. Defendant's Motion for Summary Judgment was granted. Plaintiff appeals from that ruling.

The trial court held that a cherry seed or pit found in ice cream made of natural red cherry halves was a substance natural to such ice cream, and as a matter of law defendant was not liable for injuries resulting from such a natural substance.

The uncontroverted facts in the case show that plaintiff purchased a "cherry pecan" ice cream cone from defendant's retail store in Oklahoma City, Oklahoma, on November 5, 1972. Plaintiff ate a portion of the ice cream, and broke a tooth on a cherry pit contained in the ice cream. Plaintiff notified defendant of her injury and subsequently filed this action.

There is a division of authority as to the test to be applied where injury is suffered from an object in food or drink sold to be consumed on or off the premises. Some courts hold there is no breach of implied warranty on the part of a restaurant if the object in the food was "natural" to the food served. These jurisdictions recognize that the vendor is held to impliedly warrant the fitness of food, or that he may be liable in negligence in failing to use ordinary care in its preparation, but deny recovery as a matter of law when the substance found in the food is natural to the ingredients of the type of food served. This rule, labeled the "Foreign-natural test" by many jurists, is predicated on the view that the practical difficulties of separation of ingredients in the course of food preparation (bones from meat or fish, seeds from fruit, and nutshell from the nut meat) is a matter of common knowledge. Under this natural theory, there may be a recovery only if the object is "foreign" to the food served. (citations omitted). How far can the "Foreign-natural test" be expanded? How many bones from meat or fish, seeds from fruit, nut-shells from the nut meats or other natural indigestible substances are unacceptable under the "Foreign-natural test"?

The other line of authorities hold that the test to be applied is what should "reasonably be expected" by a customer in the food sold to him.(citations omitted).

12A O.S. 1971, §2-314 provides in pertinent part as follows:

"(1)...a warranty that the goods shall be merchantable is implied in a contract for their sale if the seller is a merchant with respect to goods of that kind. Under this section the serving for value of food or drink to be consumed either on the premises or elsewhere is a sale.

"(2) Goods to be merchantable must be at least such as

.   .   .   .   .

"(c) are fit for the ordinary purposes for which such goods are used...."

The defendant is an admitted "merchant." 12 O.S. 1971, §2-104(1).

In Zabner v. Howard Johnson's, Incorp. 201 So.2d 824 at 826, the Court held:

"The 'Foreign-natural' test as applied as a matter of law by the trial court does not recommend itself to us as being logical or desirable. The reasoning applied in this test is fallacious because it assumes that all substances which are natural to the food in one stage or another of preparation are, in fact, anticipated by the average consumer in the final product served....

"Categorizing a substance as foreign or natural may have some importance in determining the degree of negligence of the processor of food, but it is not determinative of what is unfit or harmful in fact for human consumption. A nutshell natural to nut meat can cause as much harm as a foreign substance, such as a pebble, piece of wire or glass. All are indigestible and likely to cause injury. Naturalness of the substance to any ingredients in the food served is important only in determining whether the consumer may reasonably expect to find such substance in the particular type of dish or style of food served."

The "reasonable expectation" test as applied to an action for breach of implied warranty is keyed to what is "reasonably" fit. If it is found that the pit of a cherry should be anticipated in cherry pecan ice cream and guarded against by the consumer, then the ice cream was reasonably fit under the implied warranty.

In some instances, objects which are "natural" to the type of food but which are generally not found in the style of the food as prepared, are held to be the equivalent of a foreign substance.

We are not aware of any appellate decision in Oklahoma dealing with this precise issue.

We hold that the better legal theory to be applied in such cases is the "reasonable expectation" theory, rather than the "naturalness" theory as applied by the trial court. What should be reasonably expected by the consumer is a jury question, and the question of whether plaintiff acted in a reasonable manner in eating the ice cream cone is also a fact question to be decided by the jury.

We reverse the granting of summary judgment in this case and remand the same to the District Court for proceedings not inconsistent with this opinion.

Reversed and remanded.

BOX, P.J., and ROMANG, J., concur.

Importance of the Case

The appellate court states in the opinion that it is "not aware of any appellate decision in Oklahoma dealing with this precise issue." This is called a "case of first impression." Therefore, the trial judge had no precedent to follow, nor does this appellate court. The court decides that the test to be applied is the reasonable expectation test. This means that the plaintiff has won the right to have her case heard before a fact finder to determine whether she should reasonably have expected to find a cherry pit in cherry pecan ice cream. Since this case was not decided by the highest court in Oklahoma, it has limited value as precedent. Some action by the highest court must be taken before it is clear what the law in Oklahoma is.

The court decides to "reverse the granting of summary judgment in this case and remand the same to the District Court for proceedings not inconsistent with this opinion." In "reversing", the appellate court has set aside the decision of the trial court. In "remanding," it has sent the case back to trial level for trial.

O'Dell v. DeJean's Packing Co., Inc. (1978)

O'Dell is another Oklahoma case decided by a different appellate court four years after *Williams*. This court is in a different position from the *Williams* court. Although *Williams* is not binding precedent for it, *Williams* exists and the *O'Dell* court cites it. In this case Sylvia O'Dell bought a can of oysters and made a soup with the oysters, some milk, butter and salt. When she ate the soup she fractured three teeth on a "little raw pearl" which was in the soup.

The trial court instructed the jury that the defendant would have a defense (which would excuse it from liability) if the jury found that "the Plaintiff should have reasonably expected that a pearl or pearls could have been found in a can of oysters." The highest court in Oklahoma had not ruled in any case which would have indicated that it was dissatisfied with *Williams*, so the trial judge adopts the reasonable expectation test. The issue in this case is not which test should be used, but what reasonable expectation means.

There are two terms you should know before you read the case.

> general denial—a contradiction of allegations in the pleadings of an adversary. The defendant denies the plaintiff's allegations in his answer
>
> preponderance of the evidence—standard of proof in civil cases. It means that the evidence is more convincing to the trier of fact than the opposing evidence, more probable than not that the fact finder believed one party's story.

O'Dell v. DeJean's Packing Co., Inc.
Court of Appeals of Oklahoma, Division 2, 1978
585 P.2d 399
Certiorari Denied Oct. 11, 1978

BACON, Judge.

Would one who opens a can of processed oysters purchased at the local grocery store "reasonably expect" to find a pearl? In this case appellant found a pearl and fractured three teeth in the discovery. Appellant is appealing a jury verdict in favor of the canning company which sold the oysters to the retail outlet where appellant purchased the oysters.

* * *

...On August 5, 1976, she opened the can of oysters, mixed the contents with milk, butter and salt, and began eating the soup. Suddenly, when appellant bit down she experienced "very sharp pain through the whole right side" of her mouth. She spat out the contents of her mouth and discovered "a little raw pearl." Appellant further discovered that she had fractured three teeth on the "little raw pearl," which resulted in at least 14 trips to the dentist to have the teeth repaired and capped.

Appellant filed the present suit on October 29, 1976 for breach of implied warranty, praying for $350 in dental expenses and $9,500 for pain and suffering.

Appellee filed an answer in the form of a general denial. Appellee's answer also pled assumption of risk, unavoidable accident, contributory negligence and the further defense "that a pearl can be reasonably expected to be found in oysters."

The case was tried on May 16, 1977, resulting in a nine to three verdict for appellee.

Appellant is now challenging the ensuing judgment under two propositions of error. Under the first proposition appellant urges the trial court erred in refusing her requested instructions, while under the second proposition appellant argues the verdict is not supported by any competent evidence.

...[W]e find the instructions given and requested omitted one very vital instruction; and that is, one which would inform the jury what is meant by the term "reasonably expected" — as the following discussion will disclose.

Oklahoma law includes the implied warranties that food purchased is merchantable and fit for the particular purpose bought. 12A O.S.1971 §§2-314–315. Most states, if not all, have similar laws; however, there is a division of authority as to what test or tests will be applied when a consumer is damaged by a food or drink item. Some states follow what has been labeled the "foreign-natural" test. Under this test, if the food item is contaminated by a foreign substance, the injured consumer can recover damages. Or, to state the test in the converse, if the substance in the food which caused the injury is natural to the food, the consumer cannot recover damages. Clear examples of natural substances would be chicken bones in chicken soup, seeds in fruit, or bones in meat.

Other jurisdictions follow what has been labeled the "reasonably expected" test. Under this test, if the substance which caused the damage can be "reasonably expected" to be in the food or drink, the consumer is deemed to be on guard for same and if injured the consumer cannot recover.

Until 1974, Oklahoma had never had a case wherein the substance which caused the injury was "natural" to the food served....

In 1974, the Oklahoma Court of Appeals, Division 1, handed down the case of *Williams v. Braum Ice Cream Stores, Inc.*, Okl. App., 534 P.2d 700, wherein a consumer was injured by biting into a cherry seed after purchasing a cherry pecan ice cream cone. In following the "reasonably expected" test the court said:

> "The 'reasonable expectation' test as applied to an action for breach of implied warranty is keyed to what is 'reasonably' fit. If it is found that the pit of a cherry should be anticipated in cherry pecan ice cream and guarded against by the consumer, then the ice cream was reasonably fit under the implied warranty.
>
> .   .   .   .   .
>
> "We hold that the better legal theory to be applied in such cases is the 'reasonable expectation' theory, rather than the 'naturalness' theory as applied by the trial court.

> What should be reasonably expected by the consumer is a
> jury question, and the question of whether plaintiff acted
> in a reasonable manner in eating the ice cream cone is
> also a fact question to be decided by the jury."

*   *   *

In the fast moving world today all aspects of life and law are continually transforming to keep in step with our rapidly changing manner of living. That is to say, more prepared food is bought than ever before in history. Complete meals are prepared from frozen or canned products and consumed. With such changes in demand for prepared foods so must the laws protecting the consumers change.

Oftentimes, extensive damage and even death is caused by a substance in the prepared food that is "natural" to the food in its *original state*. Thus, there seems little logic in the "foreign-natural" test. It appears the weakness in this test leads to ridiculous results. Where is the line drawn? For example, chicken bones are natural to chicken, but so are beaks, claws, and intestines. One therefore wonders what the courts in the jurisdictions following the "foreign-natural" test would decide in the chicken soup case if it were a chicken beak or claw that caused the damage rather than a chicken bone, because all three parts are "natural" to the chicken. These jurisdictions appear to focus their attention on the product in its original or natural form and not on the end product bought by the consumer. Such reasoning assumes *all substances* which are natural to the food are anticipated to possibly be in the food *ultimately purchased in processed form*. Naturalness of substance can only be important in determining whether a consumer would anticipate or expect to find the substance in the food *as served or processed*.

If one purchases a whole fish to bake surely he or she could "reasonably expect" to find bones in it. However, if one purchases fish patties or fish sticks, it seems unrealistic to say he would "reasonably expect" to find bones in the processed items.

Likewise, if one purchases oysters in the shell it might be said one could "reasonably expect" to find a pearl in one of the oysters. However, if one purchases canned processed oysters it seems unrealistic to say he could "reasonably expect" to find a pearl in same. Herein lies the difficulty or confusion in food cases. The *possibility* of finding a harmful substance versus the *probability* of finding a harmful substance seems the key in analyzing these cases. When one "expects" he looks "forward to the probable occurrence or appearance" that is considered "likely or certain."[1] So if one opens a can of processed oysters, certainly there is a *possibility* a pearl can be found but the *probability* of finding a pearl is remote. With possibility at one end of the scale and probability at the other end, it seems logical to determine that if one "reasonably expects" a "probable occurrence or appearance" that expectation leads us closer to the probability end rather than the possibility end. Another example of the end of the scale "reasonably expected" is closer to is found when one buys a prepared hamburger, for in this instance there is a *possibility* that a bone will be in it, but one does not "reasonably expect" to find one. Thus, it seems obvious that when one "reasonably expects" an occurrence or appearance, it is more *probable* than just possible.

If one "reasonably expects" to find an item in his or her food then he guards against being injured by watching for that item. When one eats a hamburger he does not nibble his way along hunting for bones because he is not "reasonably expecting" one in the food. Likewise, when one eats processed oysters, normally one does not gingerly graze through each oyster hunting for a pearl because he is not "reasonably expecting" one in the food. It seems logical some consideration should be given to the manner in which the food is normally eaten in determining if a person can be said to "reasonably expect" an item in processed food. In the present case we think the aver-

---

1. The American Heritage Dictionary of the English Language 461 (1973).

age, ordinary, reasonably prudent person eating processed oysters would eat same by way of bites and would not nibble her way through each oyster because of the possibility of finding a pearl. In fact, appellee's own witness testified as follows:

"Q. Do you know of any reason why a consumer should have to inspect your food product before he eats each morsel of it, sir?

"A. No, sir.

"Q. You don't believe that's necessary.

"A. (Shakes head.)

"Q. You know of any reason why he should anticipate finding a raw pearl in your food product?"

"A. No, sir."

In the present case, in reading the instructions given and requested, we find no definition of what is meant by the term "reasonably expected." One can easily imagine without such a definition how the jurors could be confused, with some arguing there is a *possibility* of finding a pearl in canned oysters and others arguing that although it is true there is a possibility of such a discovery, it is not *probable* that a pearl would be found. Each juror would have little idea what is meant when the term "reasonably expected" is used. In the present case the words "reasonably expected" were used in the given instructions only twice. First the trial court instructed as follows:

"The Defendant further alleges that the Plaintiff should have 'reasonably expected' to find a pearl in the oyster."

The second time the term appeared was in the following instruction:

"The Defendant has the affirmative defense of proving by a preponderance of the evidence each of the following:

1) That the oysters in question were fit for the ordinary purposes for which such goods were used,

2) That the Plaintiff should have reasonably expected that a pearl or pearls could have been found in a can of oysters.

If you find that the Plaintiff has proven what she is required to prove as set forth above and you find that the Defendant failed to prove either of the items the Defendant is required to prove, then your verdict would be for the Plaintiff as against the Defendant. However, should you find that the Plaintiff has failed to prove what she is required to prove as set forth above or in the alternative that the Defendant has proved each of the items above, then your verdict would be for the Defendant."

Under these circumstances, without any instruction as to what is meant by "reasonably expected" the jury could not avoid confusion and we cannot say the jury knew what the basic law was to be applied to the case.... We think that in preparing such an instruction in the present case consideration should be given to the fact that the term "reasonably expected" involves more of a probability than just a possibility.

The case is reversed and remanded for a new trial consistent with the views expressed herein.

NEPTUNE, P. J., and BRIGHTMIRE, J. concur.

––––––––––

Jury Instructions

This is a case that is being appealed by Ms. O'Dell citing as the error of the judge that the wrong jury instruction was given. Since *Williams* is not binding precedent for this court, it still must rule that reasonable expectation is the rule to be followed. However, much of the opinion deals with its definition of reasonable expectation, meaning the "probability" not just "possibility" of finding the offending substance. There is also a section quoting evidence given at trial. This court must decide if the jury would have come to a different conclusion if the jury instructions had included the explanation that "the term 'reasonably expected' involves more of a probability than just a possibility." Only then can it conclude that the jury instructions as given constituted "prejudicial error" and Ms. O'Dell needs a new trial.

This case gives you an opportunity to consider the concepts of defenses and burden of proof. In this case the defendant answered Ms. O'Dell's complaint by pleading defenses in its answer. The defendant is in essence saying that even if what the plaintiff says is true, I cannot be liable to the plaintiff because the law excuses me. DeJean's defenses are assumption of risk, unavoidable accident, contributory negligence and "that a pearl can be reasonably expected to be found in oysters." As a defense it means that the defendant must prove that the pearl was reasonably to be expected. It is not the responsibility of the plaintiff to prove that it was not reasonably to be expected.

Importance of the Case

If you were an Oklahoma lawyer with an implied warranty of merchantability case, this case would be very important. Although it was not decided by the highest court, the highest court refused to hear the case. You know this because there is a notation at the beginning of the case "Certiorari denied." This means that the highest court in Oklahoma decided to let this opinion stand. This may mean only that the court had more important cases to decide. However, it also can be interpreted to mean that the court is satisfied with the result in *O'Dell* and is implicitly sanctioning the reasonable expectation test itself as well as its meaning as "probability" of happening rather than "possibility" of happening. Oklahoma lawyers prepare their cases knowing that they have to argue "probability."

Law students can make much less significant use of the case. You are learning how to make legal arguments, but you are tested on your abilities on an exam, not in an Oklahoma courtroom. On an exam you are in no particular state. You cannot cite *O'Dell* as law. The most you can do is suggest in your discussion of reasonable expectation that one jurisdiction has defined it as "probability." You might suggest what your analysis of the fact pattern would be using that standard.

Casebooks

Reading Cases in Casebooks

Law students learn law by a teaching process known as the case method. The case method was first used by Professor Christopher Columbus Langdell at Harvard in the fall of 1870 in order to give students practice in analyzing cases before they became lawyers. The then prevailing method of studying law was a combination of lecture, textbook reading, and memorization.

Langdell had to create his own book in order to effectively introduce the case method. He wanted students to read nothing but original material (cases). But there was no way the law library could cope with all of his students wanting to use the same books containing these cases at the same time. Langdell's casebooks contained cases from all state and federal courts.

The case method was never a way to learn the law of any particular state. Casebooks contained cases that stated conflicting interpretations of rules since the law does not develop in the same way everywhere. Langdell considered this to be a benefit rather than a problem because it would encourage student interest in the relative merit of each of the variations of the rule. Langdell included nothing but cases in his casebooks. There were no definitions or statements of legal rules. Students were supposed to develop their own statements of legal rules after synthesizing the results of a series of cases.

The case method has changed since Langdell's time. Whereas Langdell included only influential cases in his casebooks, the trend today is to include cases which have dramatic interest, even if they do not establish a new doctrine or are not old enough to have proved their importance. Many recent casebooks have few cases in any one topic and include much non-case material such as excerpts from books or articles. Thus, some casebooks would be considered heretical by early advocates of the case method. Some of today's casebooks are nothing but a compilation of cases making clear statements of the accepted legal rules. Others are filled with cases chosen to illustrate issues on the cutting edge of the law. Others contain many cases the editors have included because they wanted to make specific, but nowhere expressed in the text, points about a particular area of law. There is no standard format for a casebook because there is no consensus about what kinds of cases should be included in casebooks; about what kind of material should be edited out of long cases to make them a reasonable length; about how cases should be arranged in a chapter; or about what supplementary material should be included.

Modern casebooks make being a law student difficult. You do not have clients' problems to guide your reading of cases as did Mr. Palmer. You are usually reading cases without a context, primarily for the purpose of learning legal rules and legal analysis. Your task in reading cases is harder than that of a lawyer reading cases. You may doubt your own intelligence when two cases which appear contradictory are placed in the same chapter of a casebook. It is likely the editor has not made it clear that one represents the position taken by most courts and the other represents a position taken by only one or that one represents a correctly decided case and the other a poorly decided one. In some instances casebook editors have edited out material that novice law students need to understand the cases they read.

Your biggest challenge is to manage the large number of pages you must read in these books for each class. Since most students assume that course books are designed to help them to learn, they react to their confusion by reading cases over and over again so that they will feel prepared for class. They don't realize that they will never be prepared for class if they feel that being prepared means that they have fully "understood" every case and come up with the "right answer" to their professor's questions. They become exhausted and depressed. Here are a few suggestions to help you avoid this problem.

1. Read something about the subject matter of the chapter or section before you read any cases.

We learn best if we have a context for our learning. Since many casebooks do not give any introduction to the area of law you will be studying, you will have to do that on your own. You can use hornbooks, commercial summary books, or the summary materials prepared for first year students by the bar review companies. Before you start reading any section of your casebook you should have a good idea of what is to come. If you know the elements of a legal rule before you start reading the cases illustrating the rule, you will save yourself a great deal of time. This is what Mr. Palmer did in Chapter 1.

Your reading also may state which are the rules for the majority of jurisdictions and which for the minority. Make note of this because casebook editors like to put a majority and a minority jurisdiction opinion together. If you know the range of rules before you start reading, you can concentrate on the important aspects of the cases—how those rules are argued.

2. Read whole sections of chapters before you take notes on any case.

The only way I made it through my law school courses was to read through the whole section of a chapter so that I could think about the role of each case in the section before I began my note taking. Often I found that the first case in any section was an old one. It contained vocabulary that was incomprehensible. After I read through the rest of the cases, I found that the first case was in the section just to provide a background for the legal theory of the section. Often it was no longer good law. I realized that agonizing over these history cases was pointless. After reading the whole section, I knew what the major point of the case was and I wrote only that for my notes. This approach might work for you as well.

If you were reading a whole section of cases on the implied warranty of merchantability, the first case might be *Mix v. Ingersoll Candy Co.* because it is considered the source of the foreign/natural test. It is quoted at great length in *Ex parte Morrison's Cafeteria of Montgomery, Inc.,* which appears later in this chapter. The case dates from 1936 and its legal vocabulary is difficult. A major portion of it refers to a commercial code which predates the Uniform Commercial Code. A casebook editor would include *Mix* because it was important in the historical development of this area of law, but you might spend too much time reading it if you didn't realize that it was just there for historical purposes. If you read through all the cases on the implied warranty of merchantability, you would realize why it was included, and when you went back to take notes you would take few.

There are many areas of the law which change dramatically at some point. Of course, this is true for every area of the law if you look at just one state. Once the highest court decides that the test of merchantability is reasonable expectation rather than foreign/natural, the preceding cases are irrelevant as precedent. Most of your courses will contain cases from all states so this will not be an issue for you in them. However, federal Supreme Court decisions change the law for everyone. Your Constitutional Law and Criminal Procedure casebooks are composed largely of Supreme Court cases. Instead of summarizing the early law and starting the case section with the precedent changing case, some casebook editors give you the whole series. I found that when I read the whole section I found the case that changed the law and when I went back to take notes on the cases, I took fewer notes on the pre-precedent changing cases and wrote more detailed notes on those after it. If you take notes on a case right after you read it, you deny yourself the opportunity of figuring out where the case fits into the development of the law.

3. Don't agonize over any case

I believe that every case should be read twice, but no more than twice. The first time you read a case is when you are reading every case in the section. You should read it quickly, looking only for the element at issue and making some kind of assessment of why the case is included. Is it a history case, a precedent setting case, a case with a good fact pattern, an especially clear statement by the judge of the area of law, a majority jurisdiction decision, a minority jurisdiction decision, a well decided case, a poorly decided case?

After you have your "take" on the structure of the section, you can go back to the beginning to read each case more carefully so that you can take notes. Some cases should get a lot of your attention, some little. Your context material may mention some of the important cases so that you will be prepared to pay the most attention to them. However, if you do not understand a particular case, forget it. In the greater scheme of things, it does not make sense for you to spend two hours trying to figure out one case. You will find out at the next class what point the editor was trying to make. You will usually discover that you never would have thought of that point.

4. Don't take too many notes

I have met with many first year students whose notes on one case may be as long as the case itself. When students do not know what is important, they write down everything.

Some professors will tell you how they want you to take case notes for their classes. This usually means that they will expect you to be able to answer questions in class on the items they specify. At some law schools some student or faculty orientation committee explains the note taking process known as "briefing" to all first year students. The traditional brief format is anything but brief. It seems to be a more appropriate format for a lawyer with a client's case in mind than for a law student. It usually includes much of the procedural information we discussed in the Cases chapter.

If you are not given a note taking format to follow in your classes, I'll give you below a short format that will focus on the information you will need to prepare your outlines to study for exams. Even if you are given a suggested format, you may find yourself at some point in the semester with not enough time to follow it. There should always be enough time to take notes if you are using my format.

Taking Notes on Cases

The format I suggest for taking notes has four major components:

1. Rule statement of the cause of action
2. Element of the rule at issue in the case
3. Short fact statement focusing on the element at issue
4. Reasoning

Precedent Reasoning

Real World Reasoning

Policy Reasoning

Some of the traditional briefing formats require a statement of the issue in the case and a statement of the decision of the court regarding the issue (holding). I have eliminated a statement of the issue because I have found that there is no consensus about just what the word means. Many professors use the word "issue" to mean nothing more than the legal theory in the case. This is how the word is usually used to describe the most common law school exam question, the issue spotter. Other professors use it to describe a statement that relates the facts to the law. For them the issue in *Webster* might be, "Does the presence of a fish bone in otherwise wholesome fish chowder make the chowder unmerchantable?" Your legal writing instructor will probably have an even more elaborate requirement for an issue statement. You have to determine just what your professors mean by "issue" and whether they want you to prepare a statement of the issue for class.

Most students who use my format say they have found it helpful, often reducing their study time considerably with no loss of effectiveness. Following are the notes for *Webster* using this format.

Rule: "A warranty that the goods shall be merchantable is implied in a contract for their sale if the seller is a merchant with respect to goods of that kind. Goods to be merchantable must be at least such as (c) are fit for the ordinary purposes for which such goods are used."

Element at Issue: merchantability

Facts: Mrs. Webster bought fish chowder at the Blue Ship Tea Room. The chowder was not tainted. She stirred the chowder before eating it. A fish bone lodged in her throat, and she required surgery to have it removed.

Reasoning:

> Precedent

> not like tainted mackerel (Mass. case)
> not like stones in beans (Mass.)
> more like California case of bone in seafood mor-
> nay and an Ohio case of an oyster shell in fried
> oysters

> Policy

> (Plaintiff) — should be high standard for food

> Real Life

> No fish chowder recipe calls for the removal of bones.
> Removing the bones would turn fish chowder into an
> "insipid broth"

Although it may seem to you a waste of time to write out the text of the legal rule for each case, you may find it helpful if you don't like to memorize or find it difficult. By the end of all of your courses, you will need to have memorized all the rules. Even if your exam is an open book exam, you will not have time to look up anything. In order to be prepared, you need to have the rules in your head (and hand) so that you can write them down without thinking about them. Writing rule sentences for each case may result in your memorization of those rules as you go through the course. Waiting until the end of the course to memorize is asking a lot of your brain.

Practice Taking Notes

The best way to see how this works is with a sample casebook section. Three cases follow that have been edited to eliminate aspects that might be distracting. First read each case once quickly. On this reading just get an idea of what the case is about and why I would want to include it in a chapter on the implied warranty of merchantability. Then go back and read each for important details.

Ex parte Morrison's Cafeteria of Montgomery, Inc.
Supreme Court of Alabama 1983
431 So. 2d 975

SHORES, Justice.

This case presents a question of first impression in this state. Morrison's Cafeteria of Montgomery, Inc., petitioned this court for a writ of certiorari to the Court of Civil Appeals following that court's affirmance of the trial court's judgment entered on a jury verdict totalling $6,000.78 against Morrison's for injuries sustained when Rodney Haddox, a minor, choked on a fish-bone while dining at the restaurant.

The facts as found by the Court of Civil Appeals and by which we are bound are as follows:

"Mrs. Haddox testified that around 2:00 or 3:00 p.m. one afternoon in May 1980, she and her three-year-old son Rodney went to Morrison's Cafeteria. Rodney wanted some fish. Mrs. Haddox took one tray and she and Rodney proceeded down the food line. Mrs. Haddox's testimony as to how she received a portion of fish almondine is conflicting. At one point in her testimony she stated that she pointed to a piece of fish and told the man behind the counter that she would take that piece of fish. At another point she stated that she asked for fried fish. At yet another point she stated that she asked for fried fish fillet. She received a portion of the fish and put it on her tray, together with another food and drink. She saw no signs advertising the fish dish. No one told her that it was a fillet or that it was boneless. She subjectively believed it to be a fillet because of its shape and her prior experience with eating fish dishes at Morrison's. When she and Rodney were seated, Mrs. Haddox cut off a portion of the fish and put it on a plate for Rodney. She testified that she pulled it apart with her knife and fork into very small pieces. At one point Mrs. Haddox testified that she pulled Rodney's portion apart to check for bones. Later in her testimony she stated that she was merely cutting it into bite-sized pieces and not checking for bones. Rodney apparently became choked on the first bit of fish. When Rodney was taken to the hospital, it was discovered that a fishbone approximately one centimeter in length was lodged in his tonsil. The bone was removed after Rodney stayed in the hospital overnight. He suffered no permanent physical injury as a result of the incident. Mrs. Haddox stated that she did not know how Morrison's could have known there was a small bone in the fish. She testified however, that the manager and other personnel at Morrison's were extremely rude to her during the course of Rodney's difficulty. She could not persuade anyone to take her to the hospital and was told at the checkout counter that she must pay her bill before she left.

"The manager of Morrison's at the time of Rodney's injury testified that the fish which Mrs. Haddox bought was Spanish Mackerel fillet. Morrison's bought the fish from Pinellas Seafood Company, Inc. (Pinellas). Pinellas ships the fish to Morrison's in five- to ten-pound boxes. Morrison's uses this fish to prepare a dish they advertise as Fish Almondine. It is not advertised as boneless and employees are instructed not to tell customers that the dish is boneless. Morrison's does not offer the fish on a child's plate because the fish does sometimes contain bones.

An employee of Pinellas at the time of Rodney's injury testified that Pinellas used machines to fillet the Spanish Mackerel bought by Morrison's. Such machines are commonly used by other wholesale fish processors. Machine filleting strips the sides of the fish away from the backbone. Using this method it is impossible to prevent the occasional presence of small bones in the fillets. Government regulations allow for the presence of small bones in fillets. The employee stated that Morrison's had not been told that Pinellas's fillets were boneless. Approximately ninety-nine percent of the fillets which Pinellas produces are sold to Morrison's, and Pinellas is aware that Morrison's in turn sells the fillets to its customers. He further testified that in order for Pinellas or Morrison's to check for bones in the fillets they would have to cut them into tiny pieces. This would destroy the fillets.

"Another witness, an employee of a fish wholesaler and retailer, stated that a whole fillet of Spanish Mackerel could be recognized by its shape."

"Mrs. Haddox brought suit on behalf of Rodney and herself against Morrison's and Pinellas to recover medical expenses and to compensate Rodney for his pain and suffering. Her complaint also contained a claim against Morrison's for false imprisonment. Morrison's filed a cross claim against Pinellas. Motions for directed verdicts were denied as to all claims except that for false imprisonment. Mrs. Haddox does not cross appeal the directed verdict in favor of Morrison's on the false imprisonment count.

"The trial court submitted the case to the jury on the theories of implied warranty of fitness for human consumption and the Alabama Extended Manufacturer's Liability Doctrine (AEMLD) against Morrison's; the AEMLD as against Pinellas, and implied warranty as to Morrison's cross claim against Pinellas.

"The jury returned a verdict in favor of Mrs. Haddox and against Morrison's in the amount of $1,000.78. Rodney was awarded a verdict against Morrison's for $5,000.00. The jury found in favor of Pinellas on the cross claim. Morrison's motions for JNOV and a new trial were denied."

Morrison's appealed to the Court of Civil Appeals, citing as error: (1) the trial court's denial of Morrison's motions for a directed verdict and JNOV against Haddox on the implied warranty and AEMLD claims; and (2) the trial court's denial of Morrison's motions for a new trial based on alleged inconsistent verdicts as to Morrison's and Pinellas. Morrison's urged the Court of Civil Appeals to adopt the so-called "foreign/natural" rule and determine as a matter of law that a bone in a piece of fish does not breach the implied warranty of fitness.

A divided Court of Civil Appeals, in affirming the trial court's decision, rejected the "foreign/natural" rule in favor of the "reasonable expectation" test. Judge Holmes, dissenting in part, agreed with the majority's adoption of the reasonable expectation test, but did not agree that the test under the present facts mandated an affirmance of the trial court.

This Court granted Morrison's petition for certiorari on October 19, 1982. We reverse.

The issue concerns the interpretation to be give Ala. Code 1975, § 7-2-314, which provides in part:

> "(1) Unless excluded or modified (section 7-2-316), a warranty that the goods shall be merchantable is implied in a contract for their sale if the seller is a merchant with respect to goods of that kind. Under this section the serving for value of food or drink to be consumed either on the premises or elsewhere is a sale.
>
> "(2) Goods to be merchantable must be at least such as:
>
> "....
>
> "(c) Are fit for the ordinary purposes for which such goods are used...."

*   *   *

The Court of Civil Appeals rejected the adoption of the so-called "foreign/natural" rule urged by Morrison's. This rule first appeared in *Mix v. Ingersoll Candy Co.*, 6 Cal. 2d 674, 59 P.2d 144 (1936), where the court, holding that a fragment of chicken bone did not render a chicken pie unfit for human consumption as a matter of law, stated:

"Although it may frequently be a question for a jury as the trier of facts to determine whether or not the particular defect alleged rendered the food not reasonably fit for human consumption, yet certain cases present facts from which the court itself may say as a matter of law that the alleged defect does not fall within the terms of the statute. It is insisted that the court may so determine herein only if it is empowered to take judicial notice of the alleged fact that chicken pies usually contain chicken bones. It is not necessary to go so far as to hold that chicken pies usually contain chicken bones. It is sufficient if it may be said that as a matter of common knowledge chicken pies occasionally contain chicken bones. We have no hesitancy in so holding, and we are of the opinion that despite the fact that a chicken bone may occasionally be encountered in a chicken pie, such chicken pie, in the absence of some further defect, is reasonably fit for human consumption. *Bones which are natural to the type of meat served cannot legitimately be called a foreign substance, and a consumer who eats meat dishes ought to anticipate and be on his guard against the presence of such bones.* At least he cannot hold the restaurant keeper whose representation implied by law is that the meat dish is reasonably fit for human consumption, liable for any injury occurring as a result of the presence of a chicken bone in such chicken pie." (Emphasis added).

59 P.2d at 148.

The undesirability of the foreign substance test lies in the artificial application at the initial stage of processing the food without consideration of the expectations of the consumer in the final product served. Surely it is within the expectation of the consumer to find a bone in a T-bone steak; but just as certainly it is reasonable for a consumer not to expect to find a bone in a package of hamburger meat. It is entirely possible that a natural substance found in processed food may be more indigestible and cause more injury than many "foreign" substances.

The "reasonable expectation" test as adopted by the Florida courts in *Zabner v. Howard Johnson's, Inc.*, 201 So. 2d 824 (Fla. Dist. Ct. App. 1967), appears to us a more logical approach. Under that test, the pivotal issue is what is reasonably expected by the consumer in the food as served, not what might be natural to the ingredients of that food prior to preparation. *Id.* at 826. "Naturalness of the substance to any ingredients in the food served is important only in determining whether the consumer may reasonably expect to find such substance in the particular type of dish or style of food served." *Id.*

*   *   *

The Court of Civil Appeals held that what a consumer is reasonably justified in expecting is a question for the jury. (citations omitted)....

*   *   *

We agree with Judge Holmes in the instant case that, on the facts presented, the Court should find as a matter of law that a one-centimeter bone found in a fish fillet "makes that fish neither unfit for human consumption nor unreasonably dangerous." (citation omitted).

Courts cannot and must not ignore the common experiences of life and allow rules to develop that would make sellers of food or other consumer goods insurers of the products they sell. As has been pointed out, "consumers do have rather high expectations as to the safety of the products which are offered for sale to them.... [and] they have a rather low threshold for the frustration of these expectations." (citation omitted).

On the facts presented here, we find as a matter of law that the presence of a one-centimeter bone did not render the piece of fish unreasonably dangerous. As Judge Holmes stated:

> "I base this conclusion on several factors that are present in this case. First of all, it is common knowledge that fish

have many bones. Furthermore, government regulations regarding fillets recognize this and allow for the presence of some bones in fillets. A one centimeter bone does not violate any of the government regulations regarding fillets. (citation omitted). Finally, it was undisputed that, in light of the process used to mass produce fillets, it was commercially impractical to remove all bones.

"I stress that my opinion is based solely upon the facts of this case. For instance, if there had been a representation that the fish was boneless or if the bone had been larger or if there had been many bones, my conclusion might well be different. Under these facts, however, I would hold as a matter of law that the implied warranty of merchantability was not breached...."

We find, therefore, that the trial court erred in denying Morrison's motions for directed verdict and JNOV....

REVERSED AND REMANDED.

TORBERT, C.J., and MADDOX, JONES, ALMON, EMBRY, BEATTY, AND ADAMS, JJ., concur.

FAULKNER, J., dissents.

FAULKNER, J. (dissenting):

I would affirm the judgment of the Court of Civil Appeals.

––––––––––

Samson v. Riesing
Supreme Court of Wisconsin, 1974
215 N.W. 2d. 662

HEFFERNAN, Justice.

*   *   *

In summary of the evidence which supports their position, plaintiffs state that it is undisputed that Pearl Samson contracted salmonella poisoning as a result of ingesting food which had been prepared by the defendants and purchased from them.

*   *   *

Neither can we predicate liability upon a theory of implied warranty. The defendant relies upon two Wisconsin cases. Doherty v. S.S. Kresge Co. (1938) 227 Wis. 661, 278 N.W. 437, and Betehia v. Cape Cod Corp. (1960), 10 Wis.2d 323, 103 N.W.2d 64. The *Doherty* case was not decided on the basis of implied warranty, but upon negligence *per se* under the statutory standard set by the Minnesota law. It is not an implied warranty case. The *Betehia* case is addressed to the question of implied warranty, but specifically holds that its ruling is confined to the situation where a patron orders and pays for a meal or food at a public restaurant.

The decision in *Betehia* is consistent with the Uniform Commercial Code, which provides in sec. 402.314 (1), Stats. (1967):

> "...a warranty that the goods shall be merchantable is implied in a contract for their sale if the seller is a *merchant* with respect to goods of that kind." (Emphasis supplied).

> "Merchant " is defined in sec. 402.-104 (1), Stats. (1967):

> "[A] person who deals in goods of the kind or otherwise by his occupation holds himself out as having knowledge or skill peculiar to the practices or goods involved in the transaction or to whom such knowledge or skill may be attributed by his employment of an agent or broker or other intermediary who by his occupation holds himself out as having such knowledge or skill."

A commercial restaurateur as in either *Betehia* or *Kresge* would fall within the definition of a merchant. Also, it should be noted that sec. 402.314(1), Stats. (1967), imposes an implied warranty, not because of the sale alone, but because of the special responsibilities that are placed upon a merchant who is defined as one holding himself out as having knowledge and skill peculiar to the trade involved. The Wauwatosa Band Mothers, although selling the food were not merchants as contemplated by the statute. . . .

Levondosky v. Marina Associates
United States District Court, District of New Jersey, 1990
731 F.Supp. 1210

COHEN, Senior District Judge:

This negligence, warranty, and strict liability action comes before the court on a motion for partial summary judgment by defendant, Marina Associates d/b/a Harrah's Marina Hotel Casino, against plaintiffs, Robert and Loretta Levondosky. Defendant maintains that there is no genuine issue of fact regarding plaintiffs' warranty and strict liability claims, and that they are entitled to partial summary judgment as to those claims.

FACTS

Plaintiff, Robert Levondosky, was a patron at defendant's hotel and casino in Atlantic City. While playing at one of the gaming tables, he ordered an alcoholic beverage from a cocktail server. The beverage was served free of charge. Plaintiff maintains that he swallowed a few thin chips of glass from the rim of the glass in which the beverage was served, and that he suffered injury therefrom. Consequently he, and his wife, instituted this action for negligence, breach of warranty, and strict liability.

DISCUSSION

*   *   *

N.J.Stat.Ann. 12A:2-314 provides that:

"a warranty that the goods shall be merchantable is implied in a contract for their sale if the seller is a merchant with respect to the goods of that kind. Under this section *the serving for value of food or drink to be consumed . . . on the premises . . . is a sale.* Goods to be merchantable must be at least such as . . . are *adequately contained . . ."*

(emphasis added). The first inquiry is whether a "sale" occurred. The statute describes the "serving for value of food or drink" as a sale. There is no doubt that defendant's employee served plaintiff, Robert Levondosky, a drink. It is less clear, however, whether defendant served that drink for "value".

Defendant was offering complimentary drinks to its patrons. Nonetheless, it was not offering these drinks out of any sense of hospitality or charity. Defendant runs a casino, and the complimentary drinks were offered as an incentive to patrons to gamble, and therefore enhance defendant's business. The statute requires that the seller be "a merchant with respect to goods of that kind." Defendant serves these drinks on a regular basis as part of its business. In fact, it would be difficult to imagine a casino without alcoholic beverages. While Robert Levondosky did not pay the cocktail server a specific amount of money for the drink in question, he was giving defendant his gambling patronage in return.[1] "It was not the intention of the framers of the Uniform Commercial Code to limit the birth of implied warranties to transactions which technically meet its definition of a sale." *Newmark v. Gimbels Inc.,* 54 N.J. 585, 258 A.2d 697 (1969).

In *Newmark* the plaintiff was injured by a hair product applied by her hairdresser. The court found that while the plaintiff was primarily paying for the hairdresser's services, there was still an implied warranty as to the hair products. When the plaintiff paid for the service, she also paid for the product. That sale gave rise to an implied warranty. In this case, Robert Levondosky paid for the drink when he purchased the services provided by the casino. When he purchased "chips" from the casino in order

---

1. It is common knowledge the casinos are not charitable institutions, and the odds at the gambling tables are set in their favor.

to gamble, he was "buying" the gambling services as well as all the incidentals that came with it. We therefore find there was a "sale" for purposes of an implied warranty.

Defendant argues that finding a sale in this instance, would unduly broaden liability under implied warranty provisions. Defendant uses the example of an art gallery serving free wine at an opening, and an accident resulting therefrom. This case, however, differs significantly from that example. A visitor to an art gallery opening is free to enter the gallery, view the art work, have some of the wine and leave without any payment whatsoever. In this case, the casino only serves drinks to patrons who have purchased gambling chips, and are gambling. Defendant also argues that serving free drinks is like offering free parking and restroom facilities, and that finding implied warranties for these services would be unduly burdensome. Free parking and restroom facilities, however, are purely services, and as services not subject to the implied warranty provision. A drink, on the other hand, is a good to be consumed by the gambling patron.

The second inquiry is whether the defendant gave an implied warranty as to the glass as well as to the drink in it. Robert Levondosky was the ultimate consumer of the drink, but the glass remained the property of defendant. In *Shaffer v. Victoria Station, Inc.,* 91 Wash.2d 295, 588 P.2d. 233 (1978) the Supreme Court of Washington was faced with a similar situation. In that case plaintiff ordered a glass of wine and the glass broke in his hand causing permanent injury. The state of Washington adopted the identical provision from the Uniform Commercial Code regarding implied warranties as did the state of New Jersey.

In the opinion of the Supreme Court of Washington, when the "Uniform Commercial Code states 'the serving for value of food or drink to be consumed either on the premises or elsewhere is a sale' and that such food and drink must be 'adequately contained, packaged and labeled as the agreement may require,' it covers entirely the situation [when a glass causes injury].... The drink sold includes the wine and the container both of which must be fit for the ordinary purpose for which used." *Id*. We agree. Defendant gave Robert Levondosky an implied warranty that the drink served was fit for consumption. Therefore, defendant's motion for summary judgment regarding plaintiffs' claim as to implied warranty shall be denied....

Sample Notes

You were probably able to determine that each one of these cases demonstrated how one of the elements of the implied warranty arises in a case. The first case, *Morrison's*, is a good example of the type of case found in modern casebooks. It did not create a new legal doctrine, nor is it old enough to have been proven to be an important case. It would never have satisfied Langdell's criteria for inclusion in a casebook. However, it does have an interesting and well developed fact pattern, and it contains a good explanation of the two tests. The element at issue in the *Samson* case is "merchant," and the one at issue in *Levondosky* is "sale." The notes you might take on these cases follow. They are deliberately left unpolished, as your notes will be.

Ex parte Morrison's Cafeteria of Montgomery, Inc. (1983)

Rule: "A warranty that the goods shall be merchantable is implied in a contract for their sale if the seller is a merchant with respect to goods of that kind. Goods to be merchantable must be at least such as (c) are fit for the ordinary purposes for which goods are used."

reasonable expectation test, not foreign/natural

Element at issue: merchantability

Facts: Mrs. Haddox ordered Fish Almondine at Morrison's Cafeteria for her son and herself. Her son choked on the first bite of fish. A one centimeter long fish bone was lodged in his tonsil.

Reasoning:

Precedent

chicken bone in chicken pie (foreign/natural test — *Mix*)
reasonable expectation test Florida — no example

Policy

sellers of food shouldn't be insurers of their products

Real world

Common knowledge that fish have many bones
Government regulations allow for small bones in fillets.
The fish was not advertised as boneless. Employees were instructed not to say it was boneless.
To get rid of small bones, the restaurant would have to cut the fish up destroying the filet, which is not commercially possible.

Samson v. Riesing (1974)

Rule: "A warranty that the goods shall be merchantable is implied in a contract for their sale if the seller is a merchant with respect to goods of that kind. Goods to be merchantable must be at least such as (c) are fit for the ordinary purposes for which such goods are used.

Element at issue: merchant

Facts: Pearl Samson ate turkey salad at a luncheon sponsored by the Wauwatosa High School Band Mothers, an organization organized to give support to the high school band. The next day she became ill and was later diagnosed as having salmonella poisoning.

Reasoning:

Language of the statute.

The statute defines a merchant as one who "holds himself out as having knowledge or skills peculiar to the practices or goods involved in the transaction." The band mothers were not merchants as contemplated by the statute

Levondosky v. Marina Associates (1990)

Rule: warranty of merchantability (2-314 quoted including container)

Element at issue: sale

Facts: Robert Levondosky was served a complimentary drink by a casino cocktail server. When he drank, he swallowed chips of glass from the rim of the glass and was injured.

Reasoning:

Precedent

Newmark—Plaintiff was injured by hair product. Although mostly paying for service, the price of the product was included in the service. When Levondosky bought gambling chips from the casino, he purchased the services including the drinks which were served only to those who bought chips.

Policy

Casino said would unduly broaden liability.

Course Outlines

The advice I gave you not to obsess about notes is just as valid for outlining. Everyone may need a different approach to outlining, but everyone should end up with essentially the same product. Everyone needs a short outline of every course organized by legal theory and a one page checklist. One of the most common reasons for poor student performance on exams is that students spend so much time learning the material from their outlines that they don't leave any time for the most important part of exam preparation, writing out practice exams (covered in the next chapter).

Many students tell me that they have to write everything first (sometimes 150 pages). Then as they learn some material they shorten their outlines to perhaps 75 pages, then to 25, then to 10. Others couldn't imagine writing 150 pages. My outlines started out as 50 pages. I then reduced them to 10 pages and then spent quite a bit of time ordering the topics we covered in the courses into analysis based checklists.

Perhaps the most important item to prepare is the checklist. Since your professors probably will want to test you on most material covered in the course, it is helpful for you to have a list of the major topics the professor covered so that you can search for issues in sometimes convoluted exam questions.

In retrospect, I would now take an entirely different approach to outlining than I did in law school and reduce the time necessary to make an outline dramatically. I would approach outlining as an expansion process rather than a reduction process. As I studied each legal theory I would compose the draft rule sentence, a list of elements, and any rules for those elements. As I read each chapter I would insert the information about each case under the element of the legal rule that was at issue in the case. This is easy for people who use computers—most of today's law students. While I read the chapter, I would refine the rule and list of elements, and then I would modify my outline to reflect the changes. When I reached the end of the course, I would reduce the entries for each element of each legal rule to the bare bones necessary for study. Although this might work for me, it could be a disaster for you. You have to find your own best method.

If you were to try my method with the material on the implied warranty of merchantability, following is what your draft outline might look like before you read any cases. It consists of the rule and the elements. You would have learned about the foreign/natural and reasonable expectation jurisdictional differences from your context reading.

Implied Warranty of Merchantability (Draft Outline)

Rule: Section 2-314 of the Uniform Commercial Code provides that "a warranty that the goods shall be **merchantable** is implied in a contract for their **sale** if the seller is a **merchant** with respect to goods of that kind." The serving of food is covered by 2-314.

Merchant: A merchant (Section 2-104) is "a person who deals in goods of the kind or otherwise by his occupation holds himself out as having knowledge or skill peculiar to the practices or goods involved in the transaction."

Sale: A contract for sale (Section 2-106) "includes both a present sale of goods and a contract to sell goods at a future time. A sale consists in the passing of title from the seller to the buyer for a price."

Merchantability: Section 2-314 (2)(c) provides that goods to be merchantable must be at least such as are "fit for the ordinary purposes for which such goods are used."

Foreign/Natural Test: Under the foreign/natural test the presence of a harmful substance makes the food unmerchantable only if the substance were foreign to the food.

Reasonable Expectation Test: Under the reasonable expectation test only if the harmful substance is not reasonably to be expected is the food unmerchantable.

After you have read your cases, you will be able to figure out where each one fits into the rule and elements outline. You may want to put a lot of information for each case as you begin to summarize each legal rule. However, as you get closer to exam time you will want to shorten the information about each case to no more than a few sentences. Following is one outline of the cases you have read in this book reduced to the length you may want to use for exam preparation. (I did not use the *Williams* case because I couldn't find any compelling legal reasoning ideas in it.)

Implied Warranty of Merchantability (Outline)

Rule: Section 2-314 of the Uniform Commercial Code provides that "a warranty that the goods shall be **merchantable** is implied in a contract for their **sale** if the seller is a **merchant** with respect to goods of that kind." The serving of food is covered by 2-314.

Merchant: A merchant (Section 2-104) is "a person who deals in goods of the kind or otherwise by his occupation holds himself out as having knowledge or skill peculiar to the practices or goods involved in the transaction."

When turkey salad prepared by band mothers contained salmonella, the band mothers were not liable because they didn't fit the language of the statute—one who "holds himself out as having knowledge or skills peculiar to the practices or goods involved in the transaction." Volunteers, no special skill (*Samson*)

Sale: A contract for sale (Section 2-106) "includes both a present sale of goods and a contract to sell goods at a future time. A sale consists in the passing of title from the seller to the buyer for a price."

When patron was injured by glass in a free drink served by a casino, it's a sale because he "purchased" the casino's services by buying chips. (*Levondosky*)

Merchantability: Section 2-314 (2)(c) provides that goods to be merchantable must be at least such as are "fit for the ordinary purposes for which such goods are used."

Foreign/Natural Test: Under the foreign/natural test, the presence of a harmful substance makes the food unmerchantable only if the substance were foreign to the food.

Reasonable Expectation Test: Under the reasonable expectation test, only if the harmful substance is not reasonably to be expected is the food unmerchantable. (Might be defined as "probability" of finding a harmful substance, not merely the "possibility" (*O'Dell*))

  1. Nature of food—

     When a child choked on a 1cm bone in fish, restaurant not liable. Commercially impractical to remove bones from fish; small bones OK, but not large or many bones; well known that fish have small bones; government standards allow for small bones (*Morrison's*)

     Since everyone knows fish have bones, one has to guard against them in fish chowder. Recipe does not call for bone removal. Commercially impossible to remove bones. (*Webster*)

  2. Preparation of food

     Chicken with thick crusty batter prevents inspection of anything underneath it. (*Yong Cha Hong*)

3. Processed food

Finding pearl in can of oysters different from finding pearl in a raw oyster. Look to the expectation of the consumer for the food as served or processed, not in its natural state. As more food processed, better laws to protect consumer. (*O'Dell*)

4. Manner of eating

We don't nibble a hamburger hunting for bones. (*O'Dell*)

It may surprise you that the names of the cases are the last bit of information in each outline entry. That is because the individual cases are usually not very important. Some professors suggest that you can use the cases on an exam as a shorthand for a particular legal idea. Very few will expect you to know more than a very few important cases in detail in most of your substantive courses. The exceptions are Civil Procedure, Constitutional Law and Criminal Procedure where Supreme Court cases dominate.

Law School Exams

The Basics

Although most students think of law school exams with dread, the truth is that success on them requires the knowledge and skills required by a lawyer interviewing a new client. The typical law school exam consists of a story which may contain every problem that the professor can dream up in his or her course subject. Students are expected to spot the legal rule which governs each problem and to evaluate how closely the given fact pattern matches the requirements of the legal rule— all under tremendous time pressure.

This is very much like what Mr. Palmer had to do in the Fox case. Mr. Palmer first heard Ms. Fox's story (similar to reading a fact pattern). He then had to determine whether there was a legal theory under which she could recover (spotting the issue). The next step was to determine the elements of the legal theory which had to be satisfied and to evaluate whether the Fox situation could result in liability for The Fearless Flounder (legal analysis). Unlike Mr. Palmer, you need not worry about proving that the events happened. Your professor expects you to take each word in the fact pattern at face value.

Mr. Palmer did library research to prepare his case. In an exam situation the equivalent of his research has been done by the students in their course reading. What Mr. Palmer was able to look up, the law student is expected to know. The similarities between the work of the lawyer in preparing a case and the work of the student in an exam can be shown by turning the Fox case into an exam question. Following is the Fox fact pattern and suggestions for how you might handle it on an exam.

Exam Question #1

A completely distraught Margaret Fox, a Massachusetts resident, has called her lawyer, Nelson Palmer. Her boyfriend, Paul Conrad, had taken her to The Fearless Flounder restaurant the night before to celebrate her purchase of a new car. She ordered filet of haddock with lobster sauce. Shortly after she began eating she felt something lodged in her throat. This made her very nervous, and she went to the ladies room to try to dislodge whatever was there. When she returned to her seat, the waitress gave her bread and milk which she ate, but she felt the object was still not dislodged. Thirty minutes later she left the restaurant. After she had been home less than an hour, she became so uncomfortable that Paul took her to the hospital where she remained overnight. That morning she had a laryngoscopy and esophagoscopy performed on her. A small bone was removed, after which her throat was very rough. Is the restaurant liable under the implied warranty of merchantability?

Law school professors have different approaches to grading exams. However, most try to use an objective method so that they can be fair to the large number of students they may have in any class. Most adopt some version of a score sheet. All professors carefully craft their exam questions to include sentences that should clue you that a particular legal theory is involved and which elements of that legal theory are at issue. Some professors feel strongly that students should be able to formulate good rule statements, and they will award points for rule statements in an answer. Each element of a legal theory will not be equally at issue in the fact pattern. Therefore, the professor will allocate a different number of points for each el-

ement. You can see that on a small scale in my score sheet for
this question.

Notice that a student will get six points out of a possible 20
just for stating the rules. This may seem a lot of credit just for
rules especially when I tell you that early in the course this
book is based on I have given out model answers for students
to follow. I am very concerned that students know rules since
law is a rule based discipline.

I require students to write the text of the UCC provision
(but not memorize it) because code courses concentrate heavily
on interpretation of specific words. Having the provision written on an exam makes it easier for both student and professor
to concentrate on the analysis. In most of your first year
courses, you will need to find and learn legal rules.

Score Sheet for Margaret Fox Question

	Rule	Analysis
Implied warranty of merchantability	1	
Sale	1	2
Merchant	1	2
Merchantable	1	
Foreign/natural	1	2
Reasonable Expectation	1	8

The rules in the following answers are in bold face. look for
arguments in these answers that were used in the cases and included in the outline.

Answer 1

**Section 2-314 of the Uniform Commercial Code
provides that "a warranty that the goods shall be
merchantable is implied in a contract for their sale
if the seller is a merchant with respect to goods of
that kind." The serving of food is covered by 2-314.**

**A merchant (Section 2-104) is "a person who
deals in goods of the kind or otherwise by his oc-**

cupation holds himself out as having knowledge or skill peculiar to the practices or goods involved in the transaction." There is no question that The Fearless Flounder would be considered a merchant with respect to food since it is a restaurant.

A contract for sale (Section 2-106) "includes both a present sale of goods and a contract to sell goods at a future time. A sale consists in the passing of the title from the seller to the buyer for a price." There is also no question that there was a sale since the meal was purchased.

Therefore, the fish filet is covered by the implied warranty of merchantability, and the only issue is whether it is merchantable.

Section 2-314 (2)(c) provides that goods to be merchantable must be at least such as are "fit for the ordinary purposes for which such goods are used." In the case of substances found in otherwise wholesome food, there are two tests used by courts to determine whether the food is merchantable.

A minority of jurisdictions employ the foreign/natural test. Under this test, the presence of a harmful substance makes the food unmerchantable only if the substance is foreign to the food. A piece of fish in which a fish bone was found would be merchantable as a matter of law. Therefore, in these jurisdictions The Fearless Flounder would not be liable.

The majority of jurisdictions employ the reasonable expectation test. Under this test only if the harmful substance is not reasonably to be expected is the food unmerchantable. In this case the merchantability of a piece of fish in which a fish bone was found would be determined by whether a person would reasonably expect to find a fish bone in fish filet. Although it could be argued that every fish has bones spread throughout making it difficult to remove all of them, in this case The Fearless Flounder chose to describe its fish as "filet," which means boneless. If it had not wanted the consumer to expect boneless fish, it should not have called it "filet." Moreover, the restaurant served the fish with lobster sauce. It would be unreasonable to expect a diner to scrape the sauce off the fish looking for bones. With this preparation, the diner would expect that the restaurant had ensured that there were no bones. A person would not reasonably expect to find bones in filet of fish with lobster sauce. The Fearless Flounder would be liable.

Answer 2

Section 2-314 of the Uniform Commercial Code provides that "a warranty that the goods shall be merchantable is implied in a contract for their sale if the seller is a merchant with respect to goods of that kind." The serving of food is covered by 2-314.

A merchant (Section 2-104) is "a person who deals in goods of the kind or otherwise by his occupation holds himself out as having knowledge or skill peculiar to the practices or goods involved in the transaction." There is no question that The Fearless Flounder would be considered a merchant with respect to food since it is a restaurant.

A contract for sale (Section 2-106) "includes both a present sale of goods and a contract to sell goods at a future time. A sale consists in the passing of the title from the seller to the buyer for a price." There is also no question that there was a sale since the meal was purchased.

Therefore, the fish filet is covered by the implied warranty of merchantability, and the only issue is whether it is merchantable.

Section 2-314 (2)(c) provides that goods to be merchantable must be at least such as are "fit for the ordinary purposes for which such goods are

used." In the case of substances found in otherwise wholesome food, there are two tests used by courts to determine whether the food is merchantable.

A minority of jurisdictions employ the foreign/natural test. Under this test, the presence of a harmful substance would make the food unmerchantable only if the substance were foreign to the food. A piece of fish in which a fish bone was found would be merchantable as a matter of law. Therefore, in these jurisdictions The Fearless Flounder would not be liable.

The majority of jurisdictions employ the reasonable expectation test. Under this test only if the harmful substance is not reasonably to be expected is the food unmerchantable. In this case the merchantability of a piece of fish in which a fish bone was found would be determined by whether a person would reasonably expect to find a fish bone in fish filet. Everyone knows that every fish has many small bones spread throughout. For a restaurant to remove all bones would require that it flake the fish, and there could be no solid piece of fish sold. The reasonable consumer knows that the restaurant uses the word "filet" to distinguish the dish from fish "steak," which usually contains a large piece of bone. Anyone who eats fish expects bones and needs to be ever vigilant to guard against ingesting same. In this case the diner need only take care in chewing the fish to protect himself from injury. A person would reasonably expect to find bones in any fish dish. Therefore, the Fearless Flounder would not be liable.

Although these two answers came to very different conclusions about liability, they were identical right down to the last section. There is no question that The Fearless Flounder is a merchant. There is no question that there was a sale. There also is no question what the result would be if the case were brought in a foreign/natural jurisdiction. The only issue is the result in a reasonable expectation jurisdiction. This is why there are more points on the score sheet for reasonable expectation analysis than for anything else.

You may have heard that law school exams have no right answers. That is somewhat of an overstatement. Here you have to know the rule for the implied warranty of merchantability, you have to know the elements and their rules, and you have to know what would happen in a foreign/natural jurisdiction. These have to be "right." What there is no "right" answer to is your finding on liability in a reasonable expectation jurisdiction. You would get as much credit for the second answer as for the first. You can make your own evaluation of the situation and argue your conviction.

The structure of the answers in this chapter is a modification of a standard format for legal analysis which consists of Issue, Rule, Analysis, Conclusion, or IRAC. IRAC is the format for legal analysis used in many legal writing courses. However, I do not find it a good format for an exam answer. You do not have time in an exam setting to do the careful crafting required by the format.

You may find that your professors want a specific format for exam writing. If so, of course you will use their formats. However, if none is specified, the format I suggest is one you can probably adapt to all of your courses.

The first task for students on an issue-spotter exam, as for a lawyer interviewing a client, is to determine what cause of action might apply to the situation and what its requirements are. Therefore, the first paragraph of all the answers in this chapter is the Rule for the implied warranty of merchantability.

The second and third paragraphs of the Margaret Fox answer discuss the elements of the implied warranty of merchantability that are not at Issue. Each of these short paragraphs contains a Rule, Analysis, and Conclusion. The Analysis consists merely of words from a fact pattern that indicate that the element is not at issue.

The remaining paragraphs of the answer discuss the element that is at Issue, the element of merchantability. The longest paragraph, and the one with the most points, is the one devoted to Analysis and Conclusion in a reasonable expectation jurisdiction.

On law school exams you are demonstrating your abilities to make the arguments that must be made for clients in areas where the law is not clear. Therefore, the model answer provides for either conclusion. Law school exam fact patterns are usually assumed to have occurred in no particular jurisdiction so that answers to questions sometimes need to include all possible approaches courts have used to treat the issue. Here, both the foreign/natural and reasonable expectation test must be discussed.

Following is a question for you to practice writing about the law. As in real life, it is not exactly like anything you have read before. It requires that you make a decision about chicken bones in chicken pie.

Exam Question #2

Donna Olson was tired. She had had a bad day at the office and was not looking forward to cooking dinner that night. As she stopped at a red light she noticed a new catering business on the corner. In the window was a large sign advertising take-out chicken pies. This was the answer! She parked the car and went into the shop of Friendly Foods Catering ("Friendly"). When she asked what was in the chicken pies she was told they contained bite-sized chunks of white meat chicken, cubed potatoes, carrots and peas. She bought a pie and took it home. By the time all the children had arrived, the meal was ready. The television set was turned on for the evening news and the family began to eat. Mrs. Olson was getting angrier and angrier over the latest political scandal when suddenly she felt a sharp object in her throat and had trouble breathing. Her children got her to the hospital where she underwent surgery for the removal of what turned out to be a chicken bone. During discovery it was learned that chicken pie recipes (including the one used by Friendly) call for boneless chicken and that Friendly ordered boneless chicken from its supplier. Is Friendly liable for breach of the implied warranty of merchantability?

Your first step should be to determine which words in the fact pattern are there to clue you that certain elements of the implied warranty of merchantability are clearly present and others are not. Although you may find it hard to believe, you should spend a large portion of the time allotted for an exam question constructing your notes. Law school fact patterns are carefully written, and it is easy to read too quickly and miss something very important. I suggest that you try taking notes for about a third of the available time. Then go back to fact pattern and underline or otherwise mark those words you have already used to buttress your arguments (I have italicized them). If there are sentences left, you must decide whether the words are there to advance the story or whether they have legal significance. Some words may be included in order to try to get you to bite at a red herring.

Notes for Answer

Rule: Implied Warranty of Merchantability

Section 2-314 of the Uniform Commercial Code provides that "a warranty that the goods shall be merchantable is implied in a contract for their sale if the seller is a merchant with respect to goods of that kind. Goods to be merchantable must be at least such as (c) are fit for the ordinary purposes for which such goods are used." The serving of food is covered by this section.

Sale — "She bought a pie"

Merchant — Friendly Foods Catering Co. — sign in window advertising the chicken pies

Merchantability

Foreign/Natural — Chicken bone natural to chicken

Reasonable expectation

Yes — know from experience hard to get all bones out, unreasonable to put burden on Friendly to ensure all bones are out.

No — "bite sized pieces of white meat chicken." White meat easy to debone. Gravy covering the meat and the bite sized pieces make it unlikely that the diner would think of or be able to inspect for bones — the responsibility of the catering company to make sure no bones. Recipe even called for boneless chicken.

Donna Olson was tired. She had had a bad day at the office and was not looking forward to cooking dinner that night. As she stopped at a red light she noticed a new catering business on the corner. *In the window was a large sign advertising take-out chicken pies.* This was the answer! She parked the car and went into the shop of *Friendly Foods Catering ("Friendly").* When she asked what was in the chicken pies she was told they contained *bite-sized chunks of white meat chicken,* cubed potatoes, carrots and peas. She bought a pie and took it home. By the time all the children had arrived, the meal was ready. The television set was turned on for the evening news and the family began to eat. Mrs. Olson was getting angrier and angrier over the latest political scandal when suddenly she felt a sharp object in her throat and had trouble breathing. Her children got her to the hospital where she underwent surgery for the removal of what turned out to be a chicken bone. During discovery it was learned that *chicken pie recipes (including the one used by Friendly) call for boneless chicken and that Friendly ordered bone-*

less chicken from its supplier. Is Friendly liable for breach of the implied warranty of merchantability?

You can see that many sentences were not used in the notes. Most of the sentences that are not underlined are there just to advance the story. However, there are two you might want to pay attention to. The fact pattern says Mrs. Olson was getting angrier and angrier. If you had decided that a bone in chicken pie was to be expected, then (to quote *Webster*), "she should be on guard against same." Her misfortune might be her fault since she was not "on guard." The defendant can use her conduct as a defense against liability. The other words are "from its supplier." Many students completely ignore the question, which asks for your assessment of the liability of Friendly, and talk about the ability of Friendly to sue the supplier. You must answer the question. You might want to add something about the anger into your notes and then write an answer.

After underlining the words I have already used and then reviewing the others, I find additional legal issues. The total analysis process should take about half of the time allocated to the question on the exam. If you have very extensive and organized notes, you can write very quickly. It is the person who does not take the time to organize and begins writing immediately who runs out of time at the end.

Now you can practice writing. Copy as much of the Margaret Fox exam answer as you can as a model, keeping the format and filling in the factual information from the notes you have.

The Complications

Exam Question #3
Mr. and Mrs. Gourmand, the owners and operators of a catering company, were excited. Their daughter Geral-

dine was to be married to a young man of whom they were very fond. Geraldine wanted to elope, but she consented to having a big wedding after much pressure from her parents. The catering business was not as successful as it had been, and they hoped that they would get business from the invited guests. They prepared an elaborate menu and sent out 200 invitations to their acquaintances.

Mr. Buck, the president of the local bank, was delighted to receive the invitation. He had never been to a function catered by the Gourmands, but he had heard that their food was superb. Although he did not know the young couple at all, he accepted the invitation immediately and bought several pieces of china as a wedding gift.

The wedding reception was held in the Gourmands's large backyard. All the guests were enjoying the food when they heard a scream of pain from Mr. Buck. While eating the beef tongue, he bit down on something hard which broke his tooth. The hard substance was later identified as a piece of beef tail bone. In a suit for breach of the implied warranty of merchantability brought by Mr. Buck against the Gourmands, who will prevail?

Notes:

Merchant—parents are caterers

No—daughter's wedding

Yes—dissuaded Geraldine from eloping, so to drum up business, invitations sent to their "acquaintances" not Geraldine's friends or their friends. Buck, prominent town resident, didn't know the couple.

Sale

Yes—Buck wanted to eat the Buck's food so bought the socially required present in exchange. Not important that present to children, food from the parents.

No—gift just a custom, could have gone without one.

Merchantable

Foreign/natural—tail bone in tongue, so natural.

Reasonable expectation—expect no bones in tongue, tail not even close to tongue

Score sheet for Gourmand Question

	Rule	Analysis
Implied warranty of merchantability	1	
Merchant	1	6
Sale	1	5
Merchantability	1	
Foreign/natural	1	1
Reasonable expectation	1	2

In this question, the analysis of what should be reasonably expected is much less complex than the analysis of merchant or sale. This is reflected in the number of sentences I put into the fact pattern about each element. A good rule of thumb is that the length of your answer about an element should be in proportion to the number of words in the question about that element. Following is an answer written by a student and that student's score sheet.

Answer

Under Section 2-314 "unless excluded or modified by section 2-316, a warranty that the goods shall be merchantable is implied in a contract for their sale if the seller is a merchant with expect to goods of that kind. Under this section the serving for value of food or drink to be consumed on the premises or elsewhere is a sale."

A merchant is a person "who deals in goods of that kind or otherwise by his occupation holds himself out as having knowledge or skill peculiar to the practices or goods involved in the transaction." It could be argued that the defendants were not merchants because this is their daughter's wedding, and they may have acted in their capacity as her parents in cooking food for the reception.

However, the better argument is that defendants do cater food for a living, are considered professionals in the occupation of food preparation. Therefore, because they are a catering company, they are merchants.

"A contract for sale includes both a present sale of goods and a contract to sell goods at a future time. A sale consists in the passing of title from the seller to the buyer for a price." There existed a contract for sale in that plaintiff accepted the invitation and brought gifts as consideration. A lesser argument would try to establish that plaintiff was a mere guest at a wedding. However, the better argument is that he did expect to eat. The fact that he brought gifts as consideration speaks also to the element of "sale" which is defined as "the passing of title from the seller to the buyer for a price." Plaintiff did bring something—gift in exchange for his meal which he was anxious from the onset to try.

To be merchantable goods must be "fit for the ordinary purposes for which such good are used." In the case of otherwise wholesome food, there are two tests used by the courts to determine whether the food is merchantable.

Under the foreign/natural test the piece of beef tail bone would qualify as being merchantable because the bone is natural to the beef, even though it shouldn't be there. The Gourmands would not be liable.

Under the reasonable expectation test food containing a harmful substance is merchantable if a reasonable person would expect to find it there. Although the Gourmands have a reputation of the highest order, Mr. Buck bit into a bone in a piece of tongue. I'm not that familiar with eating tongue. However, if a cow's tongue is like our own, there shouldn't be any bones in it. A piece of tongue should be meat and strictly meat. A reasonable consumer should not expect that a bone would be there.

Since there was a sale, a merchant and unmerchantable food, the Gourmands would be liable.

	Rule	Analysis
Implied warranty of merchantability	1	
Merchant	1	4
Sale	1	4
Merchantability	1	
Foreign/natural	0	1
Reasonable expectation	1	2

This student received 16 points out of a possible 20. One point was unnecessarily lost just because the rule for foreign/natural was not included. The three analysis points were lost because the student did not use all of the sentences in the fact pattern to decide whether the Gourmands were merchants or whether there was a sale. There should have been a mention of all the points in the Notes to get full credit. You must assume that every sentence in a fact pattern has legal significance and only disregard it when it is clear that its only purpose is to advance the story.

This student took the easy way out in this answer. Most law school professors make the elements at issue ambiguous enough so that it would be equally likely that a student decides that an element is not present or that it is. In this fact pattern, I tried to ensure that any student could come to the conclusion that there was or was not a merchant, was or was not a sale.

However, finding that there is no merchant or no sale in the Gourmand fact pattern presents a strategic problem. According to the way the rule of the implied warranty of merchantability is phrased, there must be both a merchant and a sale before the issue of a warranty even arises. What if the student had decided that the Gourmands were not merchants? A common mistake first year law students make is to stop their analysis when they reach such a conclusion. Once they decide that there is no merchant, they don't bother to discuss the elements of sale or merchantability. It is likely that they will get few points for their answer. If there are words in a fact pattern that suggest an element is at issue, make sure you mention it. What follows is the answer you read above but with different conclusions about the elements. Note the wording that I use to make it possible to discuss the next element.

Answer

Under Section 2-314 "unless excluded or modified by section 2-316, a warranty that the goods shall be merchantable is implied in a contract for their sale if the seller is a merchant with expect to goods of that kind. Under this section the serving for value of food or drink to be consumed on the premises or elsewhere is a sale."

A merchant is a person "who deals in goods of that kind or otherwise by his occupation holds himself out as having knowledge or skill peculiar to the practices or goods involved in the transaction." It could be argued that defendants are merchants because they cater food for a living, are considered professionals in the occupation of food preparation. However, the better argument is that the defendants were not merchants because this was their daughter's wedding, and they acted in their capacity as her parents in cooking food for the reception. Therefore, they are not merchants. However, if they had been merchants, the next issue is whether there was a sale.

"A contract for sale includes both a present sale of goods and a contract to sell goods at a future time. A sale consists in the passing of title from the seller to the buyer for a price." It could be argued that there was a contract for sale in that plaintiff accepted the invitation and brought gifts as consideration. He did expect to eat. The fact that he brought gifts as consideration speaks also to the element of "sale" which is defined as "the passing of title from the seller to the buyer for a price." Plaintiff did bring something—gift in exchange for his meal which he was anxious from the onset to try. However, the better argument is that plaintiff was a mere guest at a wedding. It is only a matter of custom that guests bring gifts. He could have attended the wedding without a gift. Therefore, there was no sale. However, if the Gourmands were considered merchants and there had been a sale, the food would have been covered by the implied warranty of merchantability. The next issue is whether the food was merchantable.

To be merchantable goods must be "fit for the ordinary purposes for which such good are used." In the case of otherwise wholesome food, there are two tests used by the courts to determine whether the food is merchantable.

Under the foreign/natural test the piece of beef tail bone would qualify as being merchantable because the bone is natural to the beef, even though it shouldn't be there. The Gourmands would not be liable.

Under the reasonable expectation test food containing a harmful substance is merchantable if a reasonable person would expect to find it there. Although the Gourmands have a reputation of the highest order, Mr. Buck bit into a bone in a piece of tongue. I'm not that familiar with eating tongue. However, if a cow's tongue is like our own, there shouldn't be any bones in it. A piece of tongue should be meat and strictly meat. A reasonable consumer should not expect that a bone would be there.

Since there was no sale and no merchant, the Gourmands would not be liable even though the food would be considered unmerchantable.

There would be other ways to deal with this issue. You will need to find one that fits every course you take. You will be expected to discuss every possible legal theory and every element of every theory that the fact pattern suggests.

Exam Question #4

The Student Bar Association (SBA) wanted to raise money to start a tuition scholarship program. The group decided that it would make coffee in the school office and sell it to students and to passersby on Saturday mornings. A committee spent several weeks researching coffee making techniques and determining the best coffee to buy. Signs advertising the coffee were put up all over the downtown area and on every school bulletin board. They read, "Take our counsel and buy your coffee from the coffee experts." On the first day of the project, the SBA officers brought the ground coffee and bottled water into their office and started to make the coffee. Unfortunately, one of the bags of ground coffee had been contaminated at the warehouse with the dreaded Java worm. The 20 people who bought the coffee made with the contaminated grounds were members of a high school group who had seen the signs and had decided to come for coffee before setting out for their planned outing at the discount mall. They all became very ill a few hours after drinking the coffee. Although all required treatment by their doctors and expensive medicine, they all recovered after three days of bed rest. One decides to sue the SBA. Is the SBA liable under an implied warranty of merchantability theory?

My Score Sheet for SBA

	Rule	Analysis
Implied warranty of merchantability	1	
Merchant	1	9
Sale	1	2
Merchantable	1	5

Following is a student answer with the student's score sheet.

Answer

Section 2-314 of the UCC provides that "a warranty that the foods shall be merchantable is implied in a contract for their sale if the seller is a merchant with respect to goods of that kind. The serving of food is covered by this section."

A sale (2-106) "includes both a present sale of goods and a contract to sell goods at a future time." There is no question that a sale took place since the coffee was "bought" by the high school students.

A merchant (2-104) is "a person who deals in goods of the kind or otherwise by his occupation holds himself out as having knowledge or skill peculiar to the practices or good involved in the transaction." The SBA members clearly are students and do not sell coffee for a living. However, by spending several weeks researching coffee making techniques and comparing coffee brands they acquired the peculiar skill that deals with coffee. The sale of coffee on Saturday mornings shows the intent that this was not a one-time fund raiser and was going to be an on-going operation weekly. The SBA also advertised in different areas, the school as well as downtown areas. In this form of advertising it read, "Take our counsel and buy your coffee from the coffee experts," so by this the SBA admitted they had a skill in making coffee. They would be considered merchants.

The only other question is, was the coffee merchantable. There is little disagreement that tainted food or food in which a nail or stone is found is unmerchantable. The coffee contaminated by the Java worm would be considered tainted. Therefore, it would be unmerchantable.

Since there is a merchant, a sale, and unmerchantable food, the SBA would be found liable under an implied warranty of merchantability theory.

	Rule	Analysis
Implied warranty of merchantability	1	
Merchant	1	9
Sale	1	2
Merchantable	0	5

This answer most completely used the sentences I wrote into the fact pattern to present an issue about the students being merchants. The obvious answer is that they are not merchants because they are students. Therefore, I had to include a lot of information about their planning to allow for an argument that they are merchants. Many students discussed the evidence for them being merchants, but they just couldn't believe that they would be considered anything but students. They believed that all advertising is known by any reasonable consumer to be mere puffery. If they discussed the arguments as thoroughly as did the person who wrote the sample answer, they would have received the same grade. The analysis is what is important.

Many people are amazed when I tell them that my students can use my model answer in an exam. They don't believe that there can be any range of scores with so much information right there. However, many students do not see the ambiguities built into the fact pattern. Sometimes they panic and can't even use the model effectively. I'll include parts of the exams of two students for you to scrutinize.

> Section 2-314 of the Uniform Commercial Code provides that "a warranty that the goods shall be merchantable is implied in a contract for their sale if the seller is a merchant with respect to goods of that kind." The serving of coffee is covered by this section.

> There is no question that the SBA did make a sale of the coffee to the high school group. There is no question that the SBA would be considered a merchant since Section 2-104 provides that a merchant means "a person who deals in goods of the kind or otherwise by his occupation holds himself out as having knowledge or skills peculiar to the practice or goods involved in the transaction." Therefore, the coffee is covered by the implied warranty of merchantability and the only issue is whether the coffee is merchantable.

This student would have the word "Conclusory" written beside the discussion of "merchant" and "sale." This is one of the most common problems with the exams of first year students. Some of you have come from backgrounds where the goal is to find the right answer. However, in law school your exam points come from showing how you got to your answer, not the answer itself. Law school exams should make you think of your math courses where you were admonished to, "Show your work!" This person got no points for the analysis of the two elements and no points for the rule of sale, thereby forfeiting twelve points.

I always suggest to my students that they practice writing and rewriting answers to implied warranty of merchantability questions. In order to make the best use of a model answer, in my class or in most of your courses, you need to practice the skill of using your materials. You cannot expect to go into the exam and write well the first time. The next sample is from a person who did not take this advice seriously. This answer represents another common first year student problem. This person has injected into the answer issues irrelevant to the implied warranty of merchantability. Another reason to be confident about rules and elements is that they determine the parameters of legal discourse. There are boundaries to your discussion. If you exceed those boundaries, you may not lose any points, but you will lose the time you could have spent discussing something within the parameters. Notice also that this person does not understand that *Samson* cannot be precedent in the precedentless jurisdiction of the law school exam.

> Section 2-314 of the Uniform Commercial Code provides that "a warranty that the goods shall be merchantable is implied in a contract for their sale if the seller is a merchant with respect to goods of that kind."

> A question that is at hand is whether the SBA would be considered a merchant under the implied warranty of merchantability theory. For the sake of what has taken place the SBA is the merchant selling the coffee. The twenty high schoolers bought the coffee from the SBA, so there is an obvious sale happening here. Another question of whether the school office is a proper place to make the coffee could be an issue, were the proper supplies and sanitation procedures taken. It is also said that a committee

spent weeks researching the coffee. This might not be enough time to get the full understanding, certainly not enough time to be called coffee experts.

Using the foreign/natural rule plays an important role in this case. Obviously the Java worm which contaminated the coffee is not a natural, but a foreign part to this coffee. This fact would make the SBA liable under this test, for it should have checked for impurities in the coffee.

Using the reasonable expectation test also would make the SBA liable for breach of implied warranty. Java worm contamination is not a reasonably expected thing when drinking coffee.

Using both the foreign/natural and the reasonable expectation test would seem to make the SBA liable. The defendants' best hope for judgment would be in the fact that it would not be considered a legal merchant. In referring to *Samson v. Riesing* there was a similar situation. The housewives who prepared the poisonous turkey salad were not considered legal merchants. Using this case as precedent, SBA would not be liable under an implied warranty of merchantability.

Probably the most important thing you can do to ensure that you are successful is to practice writing. Often you can obtain questions used in your courses in prior years. Before you begin writing, you can work with friends to ensure that you have identified the causes of action and the important facts. Then each of you can write out answers. When you compare your results, you can discuss strategies and which answers were the most successful. Exam preparation is most helpful when you make finding the applicable law a separate task from writing an answer. When you write you should concentrate only on developing the skill of writing. Of course, as you write you are reinforcing your knowledge of the law as well. Writing practice is a win/win activity.

Where You Are Now

Now this is not the end. It is not even the beginning of the end. But it is, perhaps, the end of the beginning.
Winston Churchill